Reviews for Suman's book, *Unjunked*

Soni Bhatt, Actress & Director
Unjunked is that rare cook book that one uses again and again simply
because one gets addicted to the recipes! i have foud it incredibly useful
while planning yummy low cal food for the entire family.

———————————————

Harsh Goenka, Chairman, RPG Enterprises
Just wanted to tell you what a fantastic book 'Unjunked' is. I have been trying all
the recipes one by one and all of them are truly delicious. A big thank you!

———————————————

Amrita Saraf, Interior Designer, Amber Casa
Fab book! Only cook from Unjunked - takes care of all my requirements. Superb

———————————————

Basudev Biswas, Director, Corner stone and Advertising professional
The book is a classic. It helps a foodie like me to savour the tastiest meals without
the baggage of calories and more the guilt. My wife loves the book as she can cook
one meal for the family, tasty and less calorie. Both my children love the new dishes.
The vada pav is superb and satiates our desire not to go on the streets. Great
suman! Way to go!to a Hyderabadi biryani plus quick lunch wraps."

———————————————

Savari Desai, Doctor
The best part about the book is the first few pages - they are well written and need
to be read by each one of us to understand the basic concepts of the food groups
and how to incorporate it into our day to day lives and eat right. I would definitely
recommend this book to anyone who loves different yet good home cooked food!

———————————————

Mukesh Mehta, Architect
"Unjunked" reveals Suman's talent to create a plethora creative delicious reciped
which have helped me discover the satisfaction of enjoying healthy food.

UNJUNKED

Healthy eating for weight loss

SUMAN AGARWAL

80+ Veg
Recipes

Weight
Loss Tips

JAICO PUBLISHING HOUSE

Ahmedabad Bangalore Bhopal Bhubaneswar Chennai
Delhi Hyderabad Kolkata Lucknow Mumbai

Published by Jaico Publishing House
A-2 Jash Chambers, 7-A Sir Phirozshah Mehta Road
Fort, Mumbai - 400 001
jaicopub@jaicobooks.com
www.jaicobooks.com

© **SUMAN AGARWAL**

UNJUNKED
ISBN 978-81-8495-566-8

First Jaico Impression: 2014
Second Jaico Impression: 2014

Suman Agarwal asserts the moral right
to be identified as the author of this work.

Design: Rachita Dalal

Food Photography: Pawan Manglani

Food Styling: Arati Fedane

Suman's Photography: Rohan Shrestha

Editing: Gayatri Sarang

Printed by
Kadambari Printers Pvt. Ltd.
114, Patparganj Industrial Area, Delhi - 92

DISCLAIMER
The information contained in this Recipe Book is presented solely for
informational purposes so that you may learn more about the subject.

The purpose of this book is to provide interested individuals with a general
understanding of how their bodies work. This book is not meant to be used,
nor should it be used, to diagnose or treat any medical condition. For diagnosis
or treatment of any medical problem, consult your own physician. The
publisher and author are not responsible for any specific health or allergy
needs that may require medical supervision and are not liable for any damages
or negative consequences from any treatment, action, application or
preparation, to any person reading or following the information in this book.

The Recipe Book may include opinions, recommendations, or content from
third parties, which may not reflect your views. References are provided
for informational purposes only and do not constitute endorsement of any
websites or other sources.

The author, editor, publishing consultant, and Selfcare India shall not be
held liable, nor be responsible to any person or entity with respect to any
loss or damage caused, or alleged to be caused, directly or indirectly by
the information contained in this book.

This cookbook is a labour of love and many sleepless nights. However, it would not have been possible without the support of several people.

I am highly indebted to my daughter Priyanka and colleague Anjali Kanodia for evaluating the recipes, conducting food trials and helping in the overall content creation.

Thanks to my husband, Mukul, my mother-in-law, Sharda, my daughters and my parents, Mahesh and Bimla Killa, for being a constant source of encouragement. Also, to my loving clientele at *Selfcare* for inspiring me to write this work.

Thanks to my sisters, Preeti and Raksha, for all their unconditional support.

I would also like to express my special gratitude to The Ink Pot (Pooja Shah) and its creative contributors for translating my vision so beautifully and absolutely.

Finally to my staff, Kamla and Nandu, for their dedicated help.

Diet guru and fitness expert **Suman Agarwal** is the woman behind the action at *Selfcare*, a nutrition clinic that has led thousands of people to weight loss and good health through custom-designed diets. She follows a simple philosophy: Banish the boring.

A certified nutritionist from UK's Oxford University and a qualified fitness trainer from the National Institute of Aerobics, Mumbai, it is no secret that Suman believes in a holistic approach to well-being. But being a foodie at heart with a passion for cooking, she always knew that the taste buds govern the success of any diet. She was determined to help fellow epicureans stay fit without compromising on their love for food. Her years of research have resulted in the perfect plan – one that's easy to follow for life.

Through *Selfcare*, south Mumbai-based Suman coaches clients on how to adopt her programme. Her clientele include prominent industrialists and Bollywood personalities.

Kolkata-born Suman dons several other hats, too. In 2009, she co-authored her first book, *The Don't Diet Diet Cookbook*. An amateur classical and western dancer, she also has a flair for languages and is an avid reader. A doting mum of three, she spends every free minute with her daughters and husband. That's when she isn't busy cooking up a storm in the kitchen…

Suman and I go back a long, long way.
Even in that distant past, I vividly recall her
interest on the culinary front. Food to her was
an expression of creativity. When I enrolled
for a nutrition programme at *Selfcare*, Suman's
dedication yielded fantastic results – I was able
to lose weight without compromising on taste.
So it is not surprising to me that she has chosen
to put that passion into working on fascinating
cookbooks, which fill a need felt in today's times.

As people, beyond geographies – be it Asia, Europe, the Americas – we are all going through what I term as "Food Anxiety Syndrome". Consciously or subconsciously, we are asking ourselves: Are we eating the right food? Is it a balanced diet for us and for those whom we love? Taste has always remained important, but how our diet affects our health is a constant concern for the urban masses. Naturally, there is an emphasis on food that is low in fat content, but there is also a newfound accent on vegetarianism. And that's where this book shines.

Unjunked has factored all these questions and churned out the essentials of a holistic, healthy, non-boring and enjoyable food platter. The fine, wholesome and delectable dishes that Suman offers are multifaceted in their virtues. First, they are a great way to fine-tune the family's health by planning what goes on the table, what the children find delectable and what can add more flavour to the food. Second, they stop cooking from being a daily chore and turn it into an enjoyable experience to look forward to day after day.

The hallmarks of a well-organised food guide are easy-to-make, quick, nutritious, colourful, mouth-watering recipes – Suman delivers all these and how! Her eclectic range creatively caters to every palette. Take, for instance, the steamed *dahi wadas* or the green *dhoklas* laced with spinach. These are simple combinations which are rather unusual. And a healthy diet doesn't have to mean retiring your sweet tooth. For the *mithais* and desserts, she has worked out ingredients that lend the taste but not the weight.

Every dish from the book – be it for breakfast, lunch or dinner – is doable and simple. I have previously tried out some of the recipes from Suman's first book, another delight for vegetarians, called *The Don't Diet Diet Cookbook*. *Unjunked* only goes to improve on that. I'm sure quite a few of these new recipes would win top gastronomic accolades.

While I don't foray into the kitchen every day, I do love to experiment with vegetables sometimes and dress the table with food that is appetising. And seeing our three children's eyes light up at the spread is a mother's true delight.

I have no doubt that *Unjunked* will bring the same joy to your kitchen as it has already brought to mine.

MRS. NEERJA BIRLA
Vice Chairperson,
Education Projects, Aditya Birla Group

Unjunked has churned out the essentials of a holistic healthy, non-boring and enjoyable food platter.

CONTENTS

BREAKFAST

LUNCH & DINNER

✳ Jain ● Gluten-free ⧗ Quick & Easy

Item	Page	*	●	⧗
MUSHROOM and TOFU SOUP	78		●	⧗
+ Garlic Bread	77			⧗
BAKED BEAN and TOMATO SOUP	80	*		⧗
+ Tricolour Salad	82		●	⧗
CHOLE PALAK	84		●	
+ Onion and Palak Paratha	83			⧗
BLACK DAL	86	*	●	
+ Quick Cabbage Salad	88		●	⧗
BASIC WRAP	89			
CORN and TOFU ROLL	90			⧗
MOONG and VEGETABLE ROLL	93			⧗
CHOLE and PALAK ROLL	94	*		⧗
RAJMA ROLL	97	*		⧗
TOFU PALAK ROLL	99	*		⧗
BOMBAY BHAJI ROLL	100	*		⧗
DOUBLE-SIDED EGG ROLL	102			⧗
ALOO MATAR TOFU ROLL	105	*		⧗
CHOLE TIKKI	106			
SPINACH TOFU PARATHA	110			⧗
MATAR PANEER PARATHA	112			
+ Hariyali Raita	114		●	⧗
MASOOR DAL	116			⧗
+ Mixed Veggie Paratha	115			⧗
VEGETABLE DAL DALIA	118	*		⧗
TOFU JHALFRAZIE	121		●	⧗
CURD RICE	122	*	●	⧗
USAL	124		●	
PAV BHAJI UNJUNKED	127		●	
BREAD CHAAT DETOXED	128			⧗
RICE and VEGETABLE BAKE	131		●	
PASTA and BEANS in RED SAUCE	132			
RED CHANA BIRYANI	135		●	
+ Mint Raita	137		●	⧗
EGG and MUSHROOM CURRY	138		●	
CORN RAJMA BHEL	141			⧗

SNACKS

DESSERTS

∗ Jain ● Gluten-free ⧗ Quick & Easy

Hello! First off, I'd like to congratulate you on the exciting journey you are about to begin. *Unjunked* is an epicurean's delight: Not only will it set you on the path to overall well-being and healthy weight loss, it is also filled with recipes that are a culinary treat.

As a practicing nutritionist for over a decade, I have had clients come to me with several misguided notions:
'I should not eat carbs!', 'Eating only fruits until noon is healthy', 'I must go on a detox diet and have only liquids', 'Having salad and soup will help me lose weight', 'Milk is white poison', 'I can shed the kilos by eating something every two hours.'

The list is endless! There are a number of fad diets out there and because they tend to be extreme, they do not work, at least not in the long run. Besides, your body needs a balanced diet and restricting certain food groups may have a negative impact on your health. Let's face it, we Indians love our grub. And now, you can eat all your favorite foods, minus the guilt.

In this book you will find delicious, easy-to-prepare recipes that you will want to dish up week after week, month after month, without getting bored. Also, I have been particularly careful in selecting ingredients that are easily available. My personal favorites are the *pav bhaji, ragda patties*, hakka noodles, burgers and *sev puri* – all nutritious, low-cal and whole meal, yet all drool-worthy. And the result will be nothing short of amazing. Of the 8000+ clients I have seen over the years, a majority have successfully lost weight and gained good health.

To get the most out of this book, I'd advise you to carefully read the first few sections. Through 5 *Golden Rules* and *Need to Complete*, I have explained the theories of healthy living and the basics of nutrition, followed by a *7-Day Cyclical Menu for Weight Loss*. This menu can help you lose anything between 700 gms to 2 kilos in a week. There is a detailed *Holiday Survival Guide* and an *Eating Out Guide* so that your options are not restricted to home food. *Calorie Swap* and *Calorie Count* will help you keep a tab on your calorie intake and help you work your way back on track if you do slip-up on your diet commitments. My recipes are an amalgamation of these theories with vegetarianism and the Indian methods of cooking with spices.

This book is a culmination of all that I have learnt and experienced in the past 11 years, and I hope it stays with you for many, many more...

Founder & Nutritionist, *Selfcare*

FIVE GOLDEN RULES

Simple principles for getting thin

#1

The time of a meal is as important as the meal itself

It is important to space out the four major meals of the day (breakfast, lunch, snacks and dinner) correctly. Ideally, this is what you should do:

> Wait for 4 hours between two major meals. If you must eat sooner, make sure you leave a gap of at least 3 hours.

> Maintain a 12-hour gap between your first and last meal of the day. For instance, if you have breakfast at 9 am, dinner should be at 9 pm.

> If hunger pangs strike between meals... There are certain times of the day when we tend to feel hungry – early morning (6–7 am); mid-morning (11 am); mid-afternoon (3 pm); mid-evening (7 pm); post-dinner (11 pm). At these times, your best options are: buttermilk, tea, coffee, green tea, coconut water, any fruit, freshly cut salad, dried fruits and nuts like almonds, peanuts, dates, apricots, figs, cashews, walnuts, and pistachios.

Most people end up satisfying these mid meal urges by popping biscuits, breads, dried snacks like *khakhras*, and *kurmura*. But these foods not only make you gain weight but put extra burden on your digestive system. Plus, people who indulge in this kind of snacking generally end up with acidity, gas and indigestion.

#2

The key is a well-balanced diet

Breakfast, lunch and dinner should be perfectly balanced. They should contain macronutrients, i.e. fats, proteins and carbohydrates (carbs) in the right ratio. If you miss fats and proteins even in one meal, you are playing with your health. However, if you are trying to lose weight, you can skip the carbs in any one meal of the day, not more than three times a week. On the next page, understand how the macronutrients can be simplified.

Fats
> Pure fats such as oils, butter, and *ghee*.
> Combinations of fats and protein, i.e. oil seeds and nuts.

Proteins
> Egg whites form the only pure source of proteins.
> Egg yolk and all meats are a combination of protein and fats.
> Full-fat milk is a combination of almost equal amounts of fats, proteins and carbs, making it a 'meal in a glass'.
> Pulses, though a rich source of protein, contain high amount of carbs.

Note for vegetarians: For lunch and dinner, always have two portions of protein – one of dal/pulses, and another of milk products. You should never have milk together with pulses. Instead, opt for curd/yogurt/*paneer* (as *paneer* is high in fat, avoid it when trying to lose weight) along with pulses.

Carbohydrates
> Simple sugars, honey, jaggery, sago are pure carbohydrates.
> Fruits are completely devoid of protein and fats, i.e. they contain only carbs.
> Vegetables are mostly carbs; they contain no fat, but some contain negligible amounts of protein.
> All cereals like wheat, *bajra, jowar*, rice, *nachni*, corn are high in carbs, but also contain a few grams of protein.
> All cereal-based products such as white and brown bread, pasta, noodles, *rawa, poha, kurmura*, biscuits, etc fall under the carbs category.

#3
Less is more

Okinawans, the inhabitants of a small island in Japan, live longer than any other community in the world. Do they have access to some wonder food which is making them centenrians? No. They simply follow a holistic lifestyle consisting of a good diet, regular exercise and positive thinking. One of their secret lies in what they call *hara hachi bu* which is self-imposed habit of calorie restriction.

The Hara Hachi Bu Principle

Hara hachi bu translates to 'eat until you are 80% full'. Simply put, it means you should leave some room at the end of each meal. The reason: It takes the stretch receptors in the stomach about 20 minutes to tell the brain how full you really are. Also, the gastric juices, enzymes and the acids from the foods take about 20 minutes to reach the stomach. So you will actually feel fuller 20 minutes after you put down your fork. If you eat until you are 100% full, you will go 20% over capacity with every meal and your stomach sac will stretch to accommodate this extra food.

Many clients consider putting themselves under the scalpel for bariatric surgery to reduce the size of their stomach sac. But this can be achieved naturally with strong will power and the right attitude and the *hara hachi bu* mantra.

Taming Free Radicals

When we consume calories they are burned for energy. This releases heat, creating free radicals in the process. These notorious free radicals damage body tissues. The more calories we eat, the more calories we burn, and the more free radicals we create. The fewer calories we consume, the fewer free radicals we produce – it's that simple.

The Okinawans naturally keep their calorie count low by opting for less 'calorie dense' foods. They consume foods that are high in unrefined carbohydrates and fibre and low in fat. Make *hara hachi bu* your mantra at mealtimes and you too will be on the path to good health.

#4

Foods to avoid at all costs

Certain foods can compromise your weight loss efforts, with just one helping setting you back by 3 or 4 days. They include:

> Cakes, pastries, tarts, muffins.
> *Mithais* such as *jalebi, sandesh, laddoos.*
> Ice creams, *kulfis*, cold drinks, *srikhand, kheer*, frozen yogurts.
> Melted cheese on pizza, bakes or as fondue.

> *Paneer* in any form or preparation is to be avoided completely till you are on weight loss.
> Fried foods like *samosa, bhujiya, pakoda*, dry *namkin, pani puri*, spring roll, *vada pav*, etc.
> Potato in any form, even baked or boiled is as fattening!

#5

Exercise, expend, burn – 40% of your weight loss depends on it

Twentieth century with all its glory of automation has left us more sedentary and immobile than ever. Today we spend much more time sitting on our desks or PC's, in cars, buses and trains or in chairs at home watching TV. As a result, we hardly walk around 2000 to 5000 steps a day. For maintaining fitness levels one must walk up to 8000 steps a day. While for weight loss it is necessary to walk between 10,000 to 15,000 steps a day. Slotting a walk session every day is a great way to factor this into your life. "An hour walk is about 6000 to 7000 steps, you can attach a pedometer to your body to track your steps throughout the day."

Fitness not only equals sport; it also equals activity. So here is how a little extra effort can help you increase mobility in your daily life.

the PASSIVE you	the ACTIVE you
Use the escalator or elevator	Use the stairs up to three floors
Meet a friend over a cup of coffee	Meet a friend in a park for a walk
Take a tea break at work	Take a quick walk outside
Sit while talking on the phone	Stroll while talking on the phone
Sit and play video games	Play a game of pool or billiards
Order your servants around for remotes, tea, water etc	Help yourself
Weekend movie outing	Weekend outing with a swim and sports

Unless we consciously decide to become more mobile in our everyday lives we are likely to suffer from increased levels of stress, obesity and illnesses. Give your health a boost by adding exercise to your life.

IMPORTANCE of a COMPLETE PLATE

Balance your plate to get the body you deserve

In every recipe, on the top right corner of the page, you will find the image of a plate that has been divided into four sections. This plate will either be complete, or partially complete with a note at the bottom on how to complete the plate.

What does this mean?

A 'complete plate' signifies a balanced meal, meaning you do not need any accompaniments to that dish in order to get all the right nutrients.

Every recipe in the book that is not a 'complete plate' in itself has one or more suggested accompaniments that you should have alongside to make it a nutritionally balanced meal.

It is essential to complete the plate and have a balanced meal during breakfast, lunch and dinner.

What makes a complete plate?

Protein + Dairy + Fibre + Carbs + Fats*

Although fats are not mentioned as a part of the plate, all recipes and combinations contain the right proportion of fat as is required by the body.

Why Proteins?

Most problems associated with a vegetarian diet are caused by low intake of proteins. Approximately 95% of my vegetarian clients were consuming just half their daily protein requirement. Issues arising out of insufficient intake of protein are manifold:

> Hair loss
> Low immunity
> Low haemoglobin
> Muscle loss leading to back and knee aches, spondylitis
> Low mental acuity
> Frequent cold, cough and flu
> Obesity
> Water retention
> Lackluster skin
> Weak digestion

Protein deficiency may not be detected in blood investigations, but it is symptomatic. Ideal protein intake is calculated based on gender, height, frame and age. It is a myth that one must eat meat to get enough protein. Had in the right proportions, vegetarian sources can complete our daily requirements. For vegetarians, milk and milk products are the only source of first-class protein (discussed at length on page 15). The recipes in *Unjunked* include pulses, eggs and tofu to up a vegetarian's protein intake.

Your body requires between 15% to 25% of calories from this nutrient group. Though a low-protein diet can wreak havoc with your health it is important to know that a diet excess in protein can have an equal negative effect, especially on the kidneys and bones. It is important to stay within your specific range.

Over the years, our traditional meals of *dal–chawal*, *dal–roti* and *idli–sambhar* have been replaced with pizzas, pastas, burgers and sandwiches. Keeping in mind the youth's meal preferences, we have unjunked these 'cool' foods and made them wholesome and balanced by adding pulses and legumes. Pulses, along with being rich in protein, are also a high source of soluble fibre, which also helps in reducing cholesterol and diabetes. While the percentage of protein is high, the protein quality is not of a high biological value. However, when coupled with cereal groups such as wheat, rice, maize, *jowar* or *bajra*, they form complete proteins.

Tofu is another good source of protein. You will find many recipes based around it. For those who enjoy Southeast Asian cuisines, including tofu is easy and it is a smart way to complete your plate However, tofu is best had in moderation as it is linked to thyroid problems and uterine cysts. I would not recommend more than 50 gms of tofu per person per day.

Non-vegetarians generally do not suffer from protein deficiency because foods such as chicken, fish, meat, etc are rich in protein. But these foods are extremely low in fibre and therefore non-vegetarians suffer from high blood pressure, cholesterol, diabetes, etc. They are advised to replace one non-vegetarian protein with pulses for at least one meal a day.

Why Dairy?

There is much controversy surrounding milk today. There are as many schools of thought in support of including it as an essential part of a daily diet as there are those that completely prohibit milk consumption after childhood. Based on study and research of our 8000+ clients, we at *Selfcare* are in the pro-milk camp. I have found that vegetarians who completely omit milk and milk products from their diet over long periods of time suffer irreparable damage.

Milk is often referred to as 'a meal in a glass' as it is a perfect balance of carbs, proteins and fats. It is a great nutrient package of 9 essential vitamins and minerals, including calcium, vitamins A, D and B12, protein, potassium, riboflavin, niacin (includes niacin equivalent) and phosphorus. Since milk contains phosphorous and Vitamin D, the calcium it contains is easily absorbed by the body. Milk proteins help to maintain and form tissues, because they contain most of the indispensable amino acids that the body can't produce. It also has lactose, which plays an important role in the conservation of digestive flora.

Busting common milk myths

No milk for me because I want to lose weight!

Many weight-loss programmes advise complete elimination of milk. For vegetarians, this can prove fatal. The only source of protein in a vegetarian diet comes from milk and milk products, dals, pulses and dry fruits. Though pulses are a good source of protein, they lack certain essential amino acids. Dry fruits have a very high fat content. Vegans tend to develop symptoms of protein deficiency such as low immunity, hair fall, anemia, water retention, hormonal imbalances, premature aging, declining intelligence, low energy levels, etc.

What's the smart thing to do? Opt for low-fat milk! Low-fat and fat-free milk have the same nutrients as whole milk. So instead of trimming nutrients by giving up milk altogether, you can trim the fat content of milk. For instance, though buffalo's milk is high in fat content, this can be reduced drastically by skimming it or made to be 99.5% fat-free. The American Heart Association endorses fat-free and low-fat milk to reduce fat in your diet but still get the nutrients you need every day.

I am an adult and have grown all I could. I do not need calcium anymore!

Milk is a major source of calcium, which is necessary for good health and strong bones. It is a misconception that only growing children need calcium. Adults also need calcium, albeit in lesser quantities. Dairy products have high amounts of calcium in a well-absorbed form. Though leafy vegetables like turnip greens, amaranth (chauli sag), cauliflower greens, fenugreek leaves (methi) are rich in calcium, they cannot be readily absorbed by the body.

The recommended daily allowance for calcium is about 1000 mg for adults (aged 22–40 years)*. Symptoms of calcium deficiency include weak bones, inability to take the direct draft from an air-conditioner, early onset of osteoporosis, etc. Osteoporosis and osteopenia are the major symptoms of calcium deficiency. Low levels of calcium can also cause high blood pressure, which is known to be the leading cause of heart disease and stroke. Many studies suggest that fat-free or low-fat milk, as part of a low-fat diet, may help reduce the risk of hypertension.

Adapted from Institute of Medicine – National Academy of Sciences, Food and Nutrition Board, 1998

I am lactose intolerant so I cannot have milk or milk products.
Milk contains lactose, which is a milk sugar. Like most sugars, it is broken down by enzymes in the intestinal tract so it can be absorbed as an energy source. The enzyme that breaks down lactose is called lactase. Infants and young children naturally have the enzyme. However, as we grow older, lactase begins to disappear in many people. By adolescence, it is gone in about 75% of African-Americans, Jews, Native Americans, Mexicans, and in 90% of Asians. If these individuals consume milk, they suffer from gas, bloating, cramps and diarrhea – all classic symptoms of lactose intolerance.

However, milk can be consumed in other forms, such as curd, *paneer*, etc, as these are more digestible forms of milk. Yogurt that contains live cultures is more easily digested because it contains healthy bacteria that produce lactase. Even if one is lactose intolerant, he/she may be able to handle small portions of their favorite dairy products. The gradual reintroduction of dairy products in progressively higher quantities tends to improve the ability to tolerate lactose.

Drinking milk will cause excess mucus production.
It has been suggested that milk and dairy products increase mucus production, and that avoiding milk will therefore alleviate the respiratory symptoms associated with colds. However, there is no concrete scientific evidence to support this. Milk does tend to leave a thin film-like coating in the mouth and/or throat, but this is the result of its texture and perhaps some saliva production, not mucus.

Other advantages of milk
> Milk contains compounds that are known anti-carcinogens such as conjugated linoleic acid (CLA) and butyric acid.
> Milk strengthens bones and promotes healthy weight. Milk not only helps build bone mass and maintain bone density, recent

studies have also shown that teenagers who drink milk tend to be leaner than those who don't. Milk provides a healthy alternative to soda and juices for teens everywhere.

> Milk helps keep diseases at bay. It is an extremely rich source of calcium, which can be easily absorbed by the bones. Research suggests that calcium helps protect against colon cancer, high blood pressure, recurring premenstrual syndrome, and possibly cardiovascular disease and kidney stones.

> Milk is the ultimate sports recovery drink. When it comes to refueling after exercise, new research suggests chocolate milk can be just as effective, if not more, than traditional sports drinks. Researchers found it helps athletes recover from an intense workout and is an effective exercise recovery drink to refuel exhausted muscles, allowing for enhanced future performance.

Why Carbs?

Just as water is a major component of any living organism, carbs form the mass of our daily meals. The function of carbs is to provide energy. Many of my clients come with the faulty notion that a low-carb diet is the only way to lose weight, but nothing could be further from the truth. Smartly cutting down on carbs is the key to weight loss, not completely eliminating it from our diets.

Half of our calorie intake should come from carbs. If our diet has carbohydrate deficit, our body begins breaking down muscles to supplement its need for that energy, thereby weakening our muscular structure.

List of carbs
All sugars, honey, jaggery, vegetables, fruits, all cereals such as rice, oats, wheat, *bajra, jowar, nachni*, and products of cereals such as breads, biscuits, pasta, noodles, *rotis*, breakfast cereals, *rawa, poha, sago (saboodana)*, cakes, pastries, juices, vegetables juices... the list is endless.

Why
Fibre?

Found in all fruits and vegetables as well as whole grains and legumes, fibre travels through the body without breaking down. It has no calories and is not absorbed by the body.

Fibre is packed with health benefits. It reduces constipation and helps regulate various gastrointestinal disorders. A diet rich in fibre helps prevent hemorrhoids, may lower your risk of colon and rectal cancer. If you are watching your weight, eating fibre will make you feel fuller longer so you eat less, thereby facilitating weight loss.

There are two forms of fibre
> *Soluble fibre* dissolves in water and comes mostly from oats, legumes and some fruits and vegetables. To lower your cholesterol, you need to eat a good amount of soluble fibre.
> *Insoluble fibre* does not dissolve in water and is found in wheat bran, vegetables and whole grains. Insoluble fibre prevents constipation.

Why
Fats?

We want to lose weight, we give up fats. We want to go on a healthy diet, we give up fats. High cholesterol, we give up fats. Few know, however, that fats are as essential for our body as proteins, and we cannot omit them from our daily diets, period.

Fat facts
> The cells and tissues of our body have fat as an integral part, thus accounting for about one-fifth to one-sixth of our body weight.
> Vital organs like the heart, brain and liver are protected by a sheath of fat and water that holds them in place and prevents injury. The nerves too are protected by fat.
> A layer of fat beneath the skin helps to conserve body heat and regulate body temperature, thus acting as insulation against cold.
> Fat around the joints acts as a lubricant.
> Food fats aid in the transportation and absorption of fat-soluble vitamins such as A, D, E and K. Deficiency of vitamin D increases susceptibility to cancer.

> If a young girl's body fat percentage is below normal, it can adversely affect the menstrual cycle, leading to amenorrhea (abnormal absence of menstruation).
> Not having adequate dietary fats can lead to nutritional deficiencies such as flaky skin, acne, creaky joints, hormonal imbalances and low immunity.

Understanding fats

The fat in your diet is of three different types: saturated fatty acids (SFA), polyunsaturated fatty acids (PUFA) and monounsaturated fatty acids (MUFA). There is also the most talked-about fat in recent times, omega 3 and 6, which are special types of pufa.

Cholesterol is an important part of each cell and every type of human cell produces cholesterol. It is a precursor of Vitamin D and hormones. Bile acids, needed for fat digestion, are also formed from cholesterol. During infancy and toddler stages, new tissues are formed, especially brain tissues, which need cholesterol. Hence, fat should not be restricted in the diet of children, especially up to five years of age. Foods high in cholesterol include dairy products, egg yolk, poultry, caviar, squid and meat.

Quantity and quality control

Adults between the ages of 25 and 60 can safely have 3–6 teaspoons of vegetable oil a day. This amount should be evenly distributed amongst the three main meals, i.e. breakfast, lunch and dinner. Inclusion of this dietary fat not only decreases the craving for SFA but also keeps you satiated for a longer time and controls in-between meal binges.

7-DAY CYCLICAL MENU for WEIGHT LOSS

700 gms to
1½ kgs weight
loss per week!

After understanding the golden rules and the significance of a complete plate, the next question is… What should we eat?

We have prepared a 7-day cyclical menu, specifically designed for weight loss on the following pages. It has been created for Indian men and women of average height and frame. The daily calorie intake has been restricted to 1200–1300 calories for women and 1500–1600 for men.

Therefore, the ideal weight loss formula is:

Five Golden Rules
+ Exercise
+ 7-day menu with specific quantities
= 700 gms to 1½ kgs weight loss per week!

Day 1

	Recipes from book	Women	kcal	Prtn	Fats	Men	kcal	Prtn	Fats
🕐 Breakfast	Capsicum and Tofu Toast + Tea/coffee (as desired)	2 slices	278	16	7	2 slices	278	16	7
🕐 Lunch	Moong and Vegetable Roll + Spicy Buttermilk	2 rolls 1 glass	284 36	12 2	4 1	3 rolls 1 glass	426 36	18 2	6 1
🕐 Snacks	Sev Puri Detoxed + Green tea	5 pieces 1 cup	115 0	6.5 0	3.5 0	6 pieces 1 cup	161 0	8 0	4 0
🕐 Dinner	Burrito Bowl + Spicy Buttermilk	2 cups 1 glass	355 36	13 2	6 1	2½ cups 1 glass	443 36	16 2	8 1
🕐 Dessert	Date Fudge	2 pieces	120	1	4	2 pieces	120	1	4
	Total calories		**1224**	**52**	**26**		**1500**	**63**	**31**

Women: Carbs 174 | Calcium = 968 mgs | Fibre = 9 gms | Iron = 11 mgs
Men: Carbs 216 | Calcium = 1113 mgs | Fibre = 11 gms | Iron = 14 mgs

Day 2

Recipes from book	Women	kcal	Prtn	Fats	Men	kcal	Prtn	Fats
Breakfast Oats Uttapam + Low-fat milk/curd	2 uttapams 1 glass	190 58	6 5	9 0.2	2 uttapams 1½ glass	190 87	6 8	9 0.3
Lunch Masoor Dal + Mix Veggie Paratha + Spicy Buttermilk	1 cup 1 paratha 1 glass	137 91 36	7 2 2	3 3 1	1½ cups 2 parathas 1 glass	205 182 36	10 4 2	4 6 1
Snacks Bread Roll + Green tea	2 rolls 1 cup	227 0	7 0	7 0	2 rolls 1 cup	227 0	7 0	7 0
Dinner Pasta and Beans in Red Sauce + Spinach Soup	2 cups 1 cup	286 37	13 1	5 1	3 cups 1 cup	429 37	20 1	7 1
Dessert Apple Rabdi	½ cup	152	7	5	½ cup	152	7	5
Total calories		**1214**	**50**	**34.2**		**1545**	**65**	**40.3**

Women: Carbs 186 | Calcium = 1129 mgs | Fibre = 6 gms | Iron = 9 mgs
Men: Carbs 245 | Calcium = 1394 mgs | Fibre = 8 gms | Iron = 13 mgs

Day 3

Recipes from book	Women	kcal	Prtn	Fats	Men	kcal	Prtn	Fats
Breakfast Baked Bean Savoury + Tea/coffee (as desired)	2 toasts	290	14	6	2 toasts	290	14	6
Lunch Chole and Palak Roll	2 rolls	313	11	8	3 rolls	470	16	12
Snacks Veggie Alfredo Toast + Thandai	1 toast 1 glass	109 129	5 8	2.6 1	2 toasts 1 glass	218 129	10 8	5 1
Dinner Guilt-free Hakka Noodles + Mushroom and Tofu Soup	1 cup 1 cup	174 73	7 4	6 4	1½ cups 1 cup	261 73	10 4	9 4
Dessert Chocolate Sandesh	2 halves	135	5	7	2 halves	135	5	7
Total calories		**1223**	**54**	**35**		**1576**	**67**	**44**

Women: Carbs 185 | Calcium = 1087 mgs | Fibre = 14 gms | Iron = 13 mgs
Men: Carbs 233 | Calcium = 1284 mgs | Fibre = 17 gms | Iron = 17 mgs

Day 4

	Recipes from book	Women	kcal	Prtn	Fats	Men	kcal	Prtn	Fats
Breakfast	Moong Dal Uttapam + Cardamom Lassi	2 uttapams 1 glass	225 85	9 3	6 0	3 uttapams 1 glass	336 85	13 3	9 0
Lunch	Curd Rice + Quick Cabbage Salad	1½ cups 1 cup	214 93	8 4	3 5	2 cups 1 cup	285 93	10 4	4 5
Snacks	Chickpea Chaat + Green tea	1 cup 1 cup	113 0	5 0	1.5 0	1½ cups 1 cup	168 0	7 0	2 0
Dinner	Baked Bean and Tomato Soup + Tricolour Salad	2 cups 1 cup	193 122	8 9	4 3	2½ cups 1 cup	241 122	10 9	5 3
Dessert	Fruity Praline Yogurt	½ cup	180	5	7	¾ cup	269	8	10
	Total calories		1225	51	29.5		1599	64	38

Women: Carbs 175 | Calcium = 1099 mgs | Fibre = 9 gms | Iron = 9 mgs
Men: Carbs 226 | Calcium = 1400 mgs | Fibre = 12 gms | Iron = 12 mgs

Day 5

Recipes from book	Women	kcal	Prtn	Fats	Men	kcal	Prtn	Fats
Breakfast Eggy Veggie Toast + Tea/coffee (as desired)	2 toasts	253	14	6	3 toasts	380	14	6
Lunch Rajma Roll + Spicy Buttermilk	2 rolls 1 glass	282 36	11 2	6 1	3 rolls 1 glass	423 36	16 2	9 1
Snacks Vada Pav Unjunked + Green tea	1 toast 1 cup	158 0	7 0	2 0	1 toast 1 cup	158 0	7 0	2 0
Dinner Red Chana Biryani + Mint Raita	2 cups ¾ cup	263 60	8 4	5 0	2½ cups 1 cup	329 80	10 6	6 1
Dessert Dudhi Halwa with Dry Fruits	½ cup	156	7	4	½ cup	156	7	4
Total calories		1208	53	24		1562	62	29

Women: Carbs 168 | Calcium = 1012 mgs | Fibre = 11 gms | Iron = 9 mgs
Men: Carbs 200 | Calcium = 1081 mgs | Fibre = 12 gms | Iron = 11 mgs

Day 6

Recipes from book	Women	kcal	Prtn	Fats	Men	kcal	Prtn	Fats
Breakfast Oats Upma + Low-fat milk/curd	1 cup 1 glass	156 58	5 5	4 0.2	1½ cups 1½ glass	234 87	7 8	6 0.3
Lunch Chole Tikki + Spicy Buttermilk	1 cup chole + 2 tikkis 1 glass	256 36	8 2	8 1	1½ cups chole + 3 tikkis 1 glass	384 36	13 2	12 1
Snacks Quesadilla + Green tea	1 quesadilla 1 cup	268 0	10 0	4 0	1 quesadilla 1 cup	268 0	10 0	4 0
Dinner Pav Bhaji Unjunked + Whole wheat bread + Spicy Buttermilk	1½ cups 2 slices 1 glass	196 174 36	8 6 2	5 0.8 1	1½ cups 3 slices —	196 261 —	8 9 —	5 1.2 —
Dessert Kesaria Sandesh	1 piece	107	4	5	1 piece	107	4	5
Total calories		**1287**	**50**	**29**		**1573**	**61**	**34.5**

Women: Carbs 205 | Calcium = 892 mgs | Fibre = 10 gms | Iron = 12 mgs
Men: Carbs 255 | Calcium = 992 mgs | Fibre = 13 gms | Iron = 16 mgs

Day 7

Recipes from book	Women	kcal	Prtn	Fats	Men	kcal	Prtn	Fats
Breakfast Paneer Open Sandwich + Tea/coffee (as desired)	2 toasts	260	15	4	2 toasts	260	15	4
Lunch Vegetable Dal Dalia + Hariyali Raita	2 cups ¾ cup	315 56	12 3	7 2	2½ cups 1 cup	394 75	15 4	8 3
Snacks Green Dhokla + Green tea	4 pieces 1 cup	133 0	7 0	3 0	4 pieces 1 cup	133 0	7 0	3 0
Dinner Burger Unjunked + Spicy Buttermilk	1 burger 1 glass	295 36	12 2	6 1	1½ burger 1 glass	442 36	18 2	9 1
Dessert Banoffee Pie	1 slice	160	4	4	1 slice	160	4	4
Total calories		1255	55	27		1500	65	32

Women: Carbs 197 | Calcium = 908 mgs | Fibre = 11 gms | Iron = 8 mgs
Men: Carbs 235 | Calcium = 1034 mgs | Fibre = 13 gms | Iron = 11 mgs

HOLIDAY SURVIVAL GUIDE

You can choose to eat healthy when you travel

You don't need to sacrifice good nutrition to have a good time!

We all know how tempting it can be to abandon our good sense while on vacation. We may make poor choices and relax our restraint... grabbing an ice cream cone here, a slice of pizza there. But with our guidelines, along with some hard work, common sense and planning, it should be a little easier.

Don't skip the protein group – No matter where you eat, do make sure that you include protein in your meals. (i.e. milk/curd/dal/sprouts/chicken/fish).

Don't skip meals – We need to eat every 3 hours to keep our metabolism high. Watch your portion sizes.

Avoid dehydration – Avoid over-indulging in caffeinated and alcoholic beverages. Always carry bottled water or ask for sparkling water with pieces of lime or lemon.

Plan ahead – Avoid buying high calorie snacks like donuts and chips by carrying your snacks like roasted *chana, moong,* peanuts, *khakras,* fruits etc.

Breakfast options – Avoid juices and hash browns. Opt for whole wheat toasts with baked beans/egg whites. Cereal with milk/oatmeal porridge/muesli with yogurt are good options. Tea/coffee may be included.

Holiday check list
> Walking shoes – Get plenty of refreshing activities like walking, hiking, biking and swimming. If nothing else, one can do some stretching, yoga/suryanamaskar/spot marching/exercising in you hotel room for 20–30 minutes.
> Vitamins and medications

> Snacks – Protein snacks like roasted *chana* (especially for vegetarians as protein options may not be easily available in international cuisines).

What to eat and avoid

Following is a list of menu terms divided into two categories – those you should avoid and those you should embrace. Let these be your guide when all else fails.

Avoid	Add
Buttery or buttered	Stir-fried (less oil)
Basted (melted fat on meat)	Steamed
Creamed, in gravy	Garden fresh
Fried, French fried, crispy	Poached
Rich	Au Jus (with its own juices)
Au gratin, or in cheese sauce	Raw

CALORIE SWAP

If you give in to the occasional temptation, all is not lost. Redeem yourself by following this exercise exchange and salvage your diet...

Indulgence	kcal	Exercise
2 fingers of Kit-Kat	110	25 minutes of table tennis
1 scoop of ice cream	140	30 minutes of yoga
1 regular pack of Lay's	150	35 minutes of cycling
1 large whisky soda	150	20 minutes of swimming
1 bottle of beer (330 ml)	150	55 minutes of pool/billiards
1 large vodka tonic	180	25 minutes of jogging
1 cup frozen yogurt	180	45 minutes on the treadmill @ 5 km/hr
1 small pack of fries (McDonald's)	230	45 minutes of Wii Tennis
1 samosa	250	1 hour on the treadmill @ 6 km/hr
1 aloo paratha	260	30 minutes of power yoga
1 slice of 12" cheese pan pizza (Pizza Hut)	280	20 minutes of squash
1 Mars bar	280	35 minutes of football
1 blueberry muffin	380	50 minutes of tennis
½ tub of popcorn	400	35 minutes of kickboxing
1 café mocha with whipped cream	400	50 minutes of Zumba
1 veg burger with cheese (McDonald's)	415	45 minutes of basketball
1 slice of cheesecake	430	1 hour 40 minutes of golf
1 pack of Maggi	440	35 minutes on the cross trainer
1 large red velvet cupcake	500	1 hour 40 minutes of dancing
1 brownie sundae	900	Unpardonable!

COOKING TERMINOLOGY

Diced – Cut into small cubes.

Drizzle – Moisten with fine drops of a liquid.

Grease – To coat with oil/butter.

Julienned – Cut into long, thin strips ⅛-inch in thickness.

Marinate – Coat with or soak foods in a liquid and allow to stand before cooking to tenderise and enhance their flavour.

Muslin cloth – A finely woven white cotton cloth.

Purée – Process food in a blender to form a thick, smooth sauce.

Quartered – Divided into four equal parts.

Roast – To cook with dry heat or cook in an oven.

Sauté – Fry briefly in a small amount of fat, tossing frequently.

Shelf life – The length of time a product can safely be stored before it becomes unsuitable for consumption.

Simmer – Cook food gently in a liquid at or just below boiling point.

Slit – Cut lengthwise into long pieces or strips.

Spatula – A kitchen tool with a handle at one end and a wide flat part at the other used for lifting, spreading, or stirring foods.

Splutter – Fry in oil to release flavour and change colour after a cracking sound.

Stir-fry – Fry swiftly in a small amount of fat/oil over high flame, stirring constantly to ensure uniform cooking.

Strain – Separating solids from liquids by passing through a strainer.

BREAKFAST

OATS UPMA

The flavours of traditional *rawa upma*,
with the added goodness of oat bran

Makes: 5 cups
Serving size: 1 cup
Serves: 5

Preparation time: 5 mins
Cooking time: 15 mins

¾ cup *rawa* (semolina)
½ cup oat bran
½ cup carrots, chopped finely
½ cup peas
1 medium tomato, chopped finely
3 green chillies, chopped finely
2 tbsp fresh coriander,
   chopped finely
½ tsp mustard seeds
8–10 curry leaves
Juice of 1 lemon
5 cups water
2 tsp sugar
Salt to taste
1 tbsp oil

1 Cook the carrots and peas in boiling water for 10 minutes.
   Drain and set aside.
2 Lightly roast the oat bran in a pan without oil, on a slow flame;
   set aside.
3 Bring 5 cups of water to the boil.
4 Meanwhile, heat oil in a pan. Add mustard seeds; once they
   begin to splutter, add green chillies and curry leaves.
5 Immediately add *rawa* and roast for 5–7 minutes on
   a slow flame.
6 Add the boiled carrots and peas; sauté for 2 minutes.
7 Add the oat bran and sauté for another minute.
8 Slowly add the boiling water, stirring continuously.
9 Add tomato, sugar, lemon juice and salt; cook for 5 minutes.
10 Garnish with coriander. Serve hot.

⧗ **Quick & Easy**

Complete your plate: With a glass of Spicy Buttermilk (recipe on page 153).

VALUE PER SERVING		
	Calories	156 kcal
	Protein	5 gms
	Fat	4 gms
	Carbs	26 gms
	Calcium	25 mgs
	Fibre	2 gms
	Iron	1 mg

CAPSICUM and TOFU TOAST

This easy-to-whip-up snack is the perfect way to start any day

Makes: 6 toasts
Serving size: 2 toasts
Serves: 3

Preparation time: 5 mins
Cooking time: 5 mins

2 cups (140 gms) mushrooms,
   chopped finely
100 gms tofu, diced
2 cups (100 gms) spinach,
   chopped finely
3 green chillies, chopped finely
2 spring onions with greens,
   chopped finely
1 large capsicum, chopped finely
1 cup Low-fat White Sauce
   (recipe in box)
6 slices whole-wheat or
   white bread (4"× 4") or
   french baguette
½ tsp black pepper powder
1 tsp dried oregano
1 tsp red chilli flakes
Salt as per taste
2 tsp oil

1   Heat oil in a pan; sauté green chillies and spring onions with greens for 1 minute.
2   Add capsicum; sauté for 2 minutes.
3   Add mushrooms, spinach and 1 tsp of salt; sauté for 3 minutes.
4   Add tofu and pepper; mix well.
5   Stir in white sauce and cook for 1 minute. Add salt as per taste.
6   Lightly toast the bread. Spread the mixture on toasted bread; sprinkle on some oregano and paprika. Serve hot.

✳ **Jain**: Use 1 medium tomato instead of spring onions.
⌛ **Quick & Easy**

A complete plate!

LOW-FAT WHITE SAUCE

Makes: 1 cup

1½ cups cold double toned milk
   (1.5% fat)
1½ tbsp corn flour
1 tsp powdered sugar
2 tbsp low-fat cheese,
   grated (optional)
Salt and pepper as per taste

1 Take ¼ cup milk from the given quantity, add corn flour to it and make a paste.

2 In a separate vessel, heat the remaining milk.
3 After 2 minutes, add the corn flour paste, stirring constantly to prevent lumps from forming.
4 When it reaches a semi-thick consistency, add salt, pepper and sugar.
5 Remove from heat and add grated cheese.

VALUE PER SERVING		
Calories	278 kcal
Protein	16 gms
Fat	7 gms
Carbs	37 gms
Calcium	283 mgs
Fibre	3 gms
Iron	1.5 mgs

MOCK MAYO SANDWICH

A toast of salad veggies tossed in hung curd
with a curried twist

Makes: 4 sandwiches
Serving size: 1 sandwich
Serves: 4

Pre-preparation time : 1 hr 30 mins
Preparation time: 5 mins
Cooking time: 20 mins

8 slices whole-wheat or
white bread (4"× 4")
4 cups fat-free curd, made
from 800 ml fat-free milk
(0–0.8% fat)
½ cup carrots, grated
1 medium capsicum,
chopped finely
4 tsp powdered sugar
2 tsp mustard seeds
¼ cup curry leaves
½ tsp red chilli powder
Salt as per taste
1½ tbsp oil
2 tsp butter

1   Hang the curd in a muslin cloth for 1½ hours. Remove
    from cloth and transfer to a bowl.
2   Add the carrots, capsicum, salt and sugar; mix well and
    set aside.
3   Heat oil; add 1 tsp mustard seeds. Once seeds begin to
    splutter, add half of the curry leaves. Remove from heat
    and add red chilli powder.
4   Add this to the curd mixture.
5   Divide the curd mixture into 4 equal portions.
6   Evenly spread one portion between 2 slices of bread.
    Apply some butter on both the outer sides of the sandwich.
7   Heat a *tawa* and sprinkle 1 tsp mustard seeds and the
    remaining curry leaves on it.
8   Then grill each sandwich on the *tawa* over the curry leaves
    and mustard seeds till golden brown on each side.

VALUE PER SERVING		
Calories	279 kcal
Protein	12 gms
Fat	8 gms
Carbs	41 gms
Calcium	274 mgs
Fibre	4 gms
Iron	1 mg

✳ **Jain**: Replace ½ cup carrots with ½ cup cabbage.
⧗ **Quick & Easy**

Complete your plate: With a cup of tea or coffee.

RAWA IDLI with SAMBHAR

Idlis made with semolina instead of rice,
served with a lip-smacking *sambhar*

Makes: 12 *idlis* and
   9 cups of *sambhar*
Serving size: 2 *idlis* and
   1½ cups of *sambhar*
Serves: 6

Pre-preparation time: 30 mins
Preparation time: 15 mins
Cooking time: 60 mins

Idlis

1½ cups *rawa* (semolina)
½ cup fresh curd, made from
   toned milk (3.5% fat)
1 fistful cashewnuts,
   chopped finely
1 fistful raisins, chopped coarsely
½ tsp fruit salt (Eno)

Sambhar

1 cup uncooked *toor* dal
   (yellow lentils)
1 small tomato, chopped coarsely
1 medium onion, chopped coarsely
¼ cup carrots, thick strips
⅓ cup cauliflower, small florets
¼ cup French beans, thick strips
1 small green chilli, chopped finely
2 garlic cloves, chopped finely
1-inch piece of ginger, julienned
2–3 dry red chillies
⅓ cup tamarind
½ tsp mustard seeds
½ tsp *jeera* (cumin seeds)
¼ tsp *jeera* powder
   (cumin powder)
1 tbsp *sambhar masala*
1 tsp red chilli powder
1 tbsp oil
Salt as per taste

Idlis

1 Dry-roast the *rawa* for 2–3 minutes. Allow to cool, then soak in ¾ cup water, along with cashewnuts, curd and salt for 30 minutes.

2 Add raisins. If the batter appears too dry or thick, dilute with some water.

3 Lightly grease all 3 plates (with 4 depressions each) of *idli* stand.

4 Pour water in the *idli* maker/pressure cooker. Once it comes to the boil, add fruit salt to the batter, stirring continuously for 30 seconds. Immediately pour into prepared plates.

5 Steam for about 10 minutes. (If using a pressure cooker, remember to remove the whistle before closing lid).

6 Remove plates; cool for 10 minutes. Scoop out the *idlis* using a sharp knife.

Sambhar

1 Soak tamarind in 1 cup water and set aside.

2 Rinse dal thoroughly. Add water, turmeric powder and some salt. Pressure-cook for 3 whistles. When cooled use a beater to get an even consistency.

3 Meanwhile, in a separate pot, boil carrots, cauliflower and French beans with 3 cups of water for 10 minutes; drain and set aside.

continued on next page…

RAWA IDLI with SAMBHAR

VALUE PER SERVING

Calories	284 kcal
Protein	12 gms
Fat	5 gms
Carbs	48 gms
Calcium	80 mgs
Fibre	1.5 gms
Iron	2.4 mgs

4   Heat oil in a pan; add mustard seeds and *jeera*. When the seeds begin to splutter, add ginger, green chilli, dry red chilli, garlic and onion; sauté for 1 minute.

5   Add tomatoes, 1 tsp salt and *sambhar masala*; sauté for 5 minutes.

6   Add the boiled vegetables and cook for 5–7 minutes.

7   Mash the tamarind in the water in which it is soaked, then strain to make pulp (do not discard the strained water).

8   Add the strained water to vegetables along with *jeera* powder, and combine with boiled dal. Let it simmer for a few minutes.

9   Serve hot with *idlis*.

✻ **Jain**: Omit onion, garlic and ginger.

Complete your plate: With Tomato Chutney (recipe in box).

TOMATO CHUTNEY

Makes: 1 cup

3 dry red *Kashmiri* chillies, chopped coarsely
3 medium tomatoes, chopped coarsely
½ medium onion, sliced thinly
20 gms fresh coconut, chopped finely
¼ tsp *jeera* (cumin seeds)
1½ tsp oil
Salt as per taste

1 Heat a wide-bottomed pan; dry roast *Kashmiri* chillies for about 1 minute.
2 Add sliced onions and coconut; roast for another minute.
3 Add tomato; roast for 5 more minutes. Allow to cool.
4 Add salt and grind in a blender to make a thick, smooth paste.
5 Heat oil; add *jeera*. When the seeds begin to splutter, add the tomato paste; cook till it thickens. Serve once cooled.

CARDAMOM LASSI

A refreshing and satiating beverage

Makes: 5 glasses
Serving size: 1 glass
Serves: 5

Cooking time: 5 mins

3 cups low-fat curd, made
    from 600 ml double
    toned milk (1.5% fat)
2 cups water
4 tbsp powdered sugar
½ tsp cardamom powder

1   Combine all the ingredients and mix with a hand blender.
2   Serve in a tall glass.

● Gluten-free
⌛ Quick & Easy

VALUE PER SERVING		
Calories	85 kcal
Protein	3 gms
Fat	0 gm
Carbs	18 gms
Calcium	145 mgs
Fibre	0 gm
Iron	0 mg

MOONG DAL UTTAPAM

A high-protein version of the South Indian pancake,
with a generous helping of vegetables

Makes: 6 *uttapams*
Serving size: 2 *uttapams*
Serves: 3

Pre-preparation time: 4 hrs
Preparation time: 10 mins
Cooking time: 35 mins

½ cup uncooked yellow or
  green *moong* dal (soak for
  at least 4–6 hours)
½ cup *rawa* (semolina)
¼ cup onion, chopped finely
¼ cup tomato, chopped finely
¼ cup cabbage, chopped finely
¼ cup capsicum, chopped finely
¼ cup carrots, peeled and grated
4 green chillies, chopped finely
½-inch piece of ginger
4 tbsp sour curd, made from
  toned milk (3.5% fat)
1 tbsp fresh coriander,
  chopped finely
½ tsp red chilli powder
1 tsp salt (or as per taste)
4 tsp oil

1 Heat a pan and roast *rawa* for 1 minute (without oil); set aside.
2 Rinse and drain soaked dal. Grind in a blender with half the chopped green chillies, ginger and ¼ cup of water.
3 Pour the batter into the roasted *rawa*. Add chopped veggies, salt, curd, 1 tsp oil, chilli powder, fresh coriander and remaining green chillies. Add ¼ cup water or until you achieve a semi-thick paste.
4 Heat a non-stick pan and spread ⅓ cup batter to make an *uttapam* 4 inches in diameter.
5 Drizzle ¼ tsp oil around the edges, cooking over low flame for 2–3 minutes, until golden brown.
6 Flip the *uttapam*, again drizzle ¼ tsp oil and cook until golden brown.
7 Repeat for remaining batter.
8 Serve hot with Green Chutney (recipe on page 152).

VALUE PER SERVING		
	Calories	225 kcal
	Protein	9 gms
	Fat	6 gms
	Carbs	33 gms
	Calcium	77 mgs
	Fibre	1 gm
	Iron	1.7 mgs

✻ **Jain**: Omit ginger and replace onion and carrots with equal quantities of boiled French beans and boiled green peas.

⧗ **Quick & Easy**

Complete your plate: With a glass of Cardamom *Lassi* (recipe on page 49).

PANEER OPEN SANDWICH

An easy-to-make breakfast toast of *paneer* and capsicum that'll keep you going till lunch

Makes: 8 toasts
Serving size: 2 toasts
Serves: 4

Preparation time: 5 mins
Cooking time: 25 mins

1 litre double-toned milk
   (1.5% fat)
8 slices whole-wheat bread or
   white bread (4"× 4")
1 medium onion, chopped finely
1 small tomato, chopped finely
1 small capsicum, chopped finely
2 tbsp fresh coriander,
   chopped finely
½ tsp black pepper powder
3 tsp dried oregano
3 tsp red chilli flakes
3 tsp lemon juice
Salt as per taste

1 Bring milk to the boil and turn off flame. Immediately add lemon juice and stir until milk curdles. Strain through a muslin cloth, making sure all the liquid or whey is removed. What remains in the cloth is *paneer*.

2 Preheat the oven at 160°C for 7–10 minutes.

3 Crumble the *paneer* in a bowl.

4 Add the onion, tomato and capsicum.

5 Add salt, pepper and coriander.

6 Divide the mixture into 8 equal portions.

7 Lightly toast the bread. Spread the mixture on the toasted bread. Sprinkle with oregano and paprika and bake in preheated oven for 5 minutes. Serve hot.

✳ **Jain**: Replace the onion with ½ cup chopped cabbage.
⧗ **Quick & Easy**

Complete your plate: With a cup of tea or coffee.

VALUE PER SERVING		
	Calories	260 kcal
	Protein	15 gms
	Fat	4 gms
	Carbs	40 gms
	Calcium	336 mgs
	Fibre	5 gms
	Iron	1 mg

OATS UTTAPAM

Loaded with veggies, this is a high-fibre variation
of the traditional South Indian pancake

Makes: 8 *uttapams*
Serving size: 2 *uttapams*
Serves: 4

Pre-preparation time: 1½ hrs
Preparation time: 10 mins
Cooking time: 20 mins

1 cup oats
¼ cup *rawa* (semolina)
1½ cups fresh curd, made from
   300 ml toned milk (3.5% fat)
1 medium onion, chopped finely
1 medium tomato, chopped finely
½ cup cabbage, chopped finely
3 green chillies, chopped finely
20–30 curry leaves,
   chopped finely
2 tbsp fresh coriander,
   chopped finely
2 tsp salt or as per taste
8 tsp oil

1 Combine the curd, *rawa* and oats; let stand for 1½ hours.
2 Add onion, tomato, cabbage, green chillies, coriander, curry
   leaves and 2 tsp salt to the *uttapam* batter.
3 Heat a non-stick pan and pour enough batter on the *tawa*
   to make a 4-inch *uttapam*.
4 Put ½ tsp oil along the sides and roast over low flame
   until crisp. Flip over and roast the other side with another
   ½ tsp of oil.
5 Repeat with the remaining batter to make 7 more *uttapams*.
6 Serve with Green Chutney (recipe on page 152).

⌛ **Quick & Easy**

Complete your plate: With a glass of *Thandai* (recipe on page 163).

VALUE PER SERVING		
Calories	190 kcal
Protein	6 gms
Fat	9 gms
Carbs	22 gms
Calcium	133 mgs
Fibre	2 gms
Iron	1 mg

VEGGIE DAL ROLL

Tomato, capsicum and onion filling enveloped
in a spicy wrap made with *moong* dal

Makes: 12 rolls
Serving size: 2 rolls
Serves: 6

Pre-preparation time: 4 hrs
Preparation time: 5 mins
Cooking time: 40 mins

2 cups uncooked green or yellow
   moong dal (soak for 4–6 hours)
2 medium capsicum,
   chopped finely
2 large onions, chopped finely
2 medium tomatoes,
   chopped finely
4 green chillies, chopped finely
¼ cup fresh coriander,
   chopped finely
2 tsp red chilli powder
Salt as per taste
2 tbsp oil

1   Rinse and drain soaked dal. Grind in blender with ½ cup water,
    green chillies and salt.
2   Add ¾ to 1 cup of water to the batter.
3   In a bowl, mix onion, tomato, capsicum, red chilli powder,
    fresh coriander and salt.
4   Heat a non-stick *tawa*. Using a ladle spread a thin layer
    of batter, around 6 inches in diameter.
5   After 1 minute, sprinkle ¼ cup of the veggie mixture over
    the spread.
6   Drizzle ½ tsp oil around the edges.
7   Gently lift from one side with a spatula and fold over
    to make a roll.

VALUE PER SERVING		
	Calories	253 kcal
	Protein	14 gms
	Fat	5 gms
	Carbs	38 gms
	Calcium	76 mgs
	Fibre	1.5 gms
	Iron	2.7 mgs

❋ **Jain**: Replace onions with 1 cup finely chopped cabbage.
● **Gluten-free**
⌛ **Quick & Easy**

Complete your plate: With Green Chutney (recipe on page 152) and a glass
of Spicy Buttermilk (recipe on page 153).

BAKED BEANS SAVOURY

A cheesy, garlicky mix of French beans and baked beans
served on whole-wheat toast

Makes: 6 toasts
Serving size: 1 toast
Serves: 6

Preparation time: 10 mins
Cooking time: 35 mins

6 slices whole-wheat or
    white bread (4"x 4")
½ can (200 gms) baked beans
½ cup carrots, chopped finely
½ cup French beans,
    chopped finely
1 large onion, chopped finely
1 large tomato, chopped finely
2 tsp red chilli powder
8 garlic cloves, chopped finely
20 gms low-fat cheese, grated
2 tbsp ketchup
Salt as per taste
1 tbsp oil

1   Pressure-cook the carrots and French beans for 1 whistle.
Drain and keep aside.

2   Preheat the oven at 160°C for 7–10 minutes.

3   Heat oil in a pan; sauté onion for 5 minutes.

4   Add garlic; sauté for 2 minutes.

5   Add red chilli powder, immediately mix in the tomatoes
and cook for 3 minutes.

6   Add the boiled French beans, carrots and salt; cook for
another 3 minutes.

7   Stir in baked beans and tomato ketchup; cook for another
5 minutes. Remove from heat and stir in the cheese.

8   Lightly toast the bread. Spread the mixture on the toast
and bake in preheated oven for 10 minutes. Serve hot.

⏳ **Quick & Easy**

Complete your plate: With a cup of tea or coffee.

VALUE PER SERVING		
	Calories	145 kcal
	Protein	7 gms
	Fat	3 gms
	Carbs	24 gms
	Calcium	64 mgs
	Fibre	4 gms
	Iron	1 mg

EGGY VEGGIE TOAST

Hardboiled egg whites, capsicum and baby corn
in a creamy sauce, slathered over toast and baked

Makes: 10 toasts	Preparation time: 5 mins
Serving size: 2 toasts	Cooking time: 15 mins
Serves: 5	

1 Hard-boil the eggs, scoop out the yolk and discard. Chop the boiled egg whites into small cubes.
2 Blanch the chopped baby corn in boiling water for 3 minutes. Strain and keep aside.
3 Preheat the oven at 160°C for 7–10 minutes.
4 Heat the oil in a pan; add the green chillies.
5 Add onion and capsicum; sauté for 3 minutes.
6 Add baby corn, salt and pepper; sauté for another 2 minutes.
7 Mix in the boiled eggs; sauté for 1 minute.
8 Stir in the white sauce and cook for another minute.
9 Add black pepper powder.
10 Divide the mixture into 10 equal parts.
11 Lightly toast the bread. Spread the mixture on the toasted bread and bake in preheated oven for 5 minutes. Serve hot.

⌛ Quick & Easy

Complete your plate: With a cup of tea or coffee.

10 slices whole-wheat or
   white bread (4"× 4")
8 eggs
2 medium onions, chopped finely
6 baby corns, chopped finely
1 large red bell pepper,
   chopped finely
1 large capsicum, chopped finely
2 green chillies, chopped finely
1 cup Low-Fat White Sauce
   (recipe on page 42)
2 tbsp oil
Black pepper powder as per taste
Salt as per taste

VALUE PER SERVING		
	Calories	253 kcal
	Protein	14 gms
	Fat	6 gms
	Carbs	33 gms
	Calcium	112 mgs
	Fibre	5 gms
	Iron	1 mg

LUNCH & DINNER

BURGER UNJUNKED

A mixed vegetables and tofu patty topped with
homemade low-fat mayo and spicy chutney

Makes: 5 burgers
Serving size: 1 burger
Serves: 5

Preparation time: 10 mins
Cooking time: 20 mins

1 Cook the French beans, carrots, cauliflower and peas
   in boiling water for about 15 minutes. Drain and cool.
2 To make breadcrumbs, toast the bread in a pop-up toaster
   until brown. Cool and grind to a fine powder in a mixer.
3 Preheat the over at 160°C for 7–10 minutes.
4 Heat oil in a pan. Add garlic, ginger and green chillies; sauté
   for half a minute.
5 Add the boiled vegetables.
6 Season with red chilli powder, *chaat masala*, *amchur* powder
   and salt; sauté for 2 minutes.
7 Stir in tofu, potato and salt. Sauté for another 2 minutes,
   then set aside to cool.
8 Finally, add the bread crumbs and combine. Divide into
   5 equal burger patties. Roast the patties on a non-stick
   pan using a small amount of oil.
9 Slice the burger buns into half and warm them in the
   preheated oven for 2 minutes.
10 On each of the lower halves, place 1 patty, 1 lettuce leaf,
   1 tbsp of Low-fat Mayo and slices of onion, tomato and
   capsicum. Cover with the other half of the bun and serve
   with tomato ketchup.

Complete your plate: With a glass of low-fat cold coffee.

5 large burger buns
½ cup French beans, chopped finely
½ cup carrots, chopped finely
½ cup cauliflower, chopped finely
½ cup green peas
100 gms tofu, grated
1 large potato, boiled and grated
1½ slices white bread (4"× 4")
   (for breadcrumbs)
3 green chillies, chopped finely
2 garlic cloves, chopped finely
1-inch piece of ginger,
   chopped finely
½ tsp red chilli powder
1 tsp *amchur* powder
   (dried mango powder)
1 tsp *chaat masala*
Salt as per taste
2 tsp oil

Serving
5 lettuce leaves (optional)
5 large slices of onion
5 large slices of tomato
5 large slices of capsicum
¼ cup Low-Fat Mayo
   (recipe on page 109)

VALUE PER SERVING		
	Calories	295 kcal
	Protein	12 gms
	Fat	6 gms
	Carbs	49 gms
	Calcium	109 mgs
	Fibre	2 gms
	Iron	1 mg

BURRITO BOWL

Piquant beans served on a bed of corn-capsicum rice,
topped with sour cream and a tangy salsa

Makes: 5 cups beans and
      6 cups rice
Serving size: ¾ cup beans and
      1 cup rice
Serves 6

Pre-preparation time: 6–8 hrs
Preparation time: 20 mins
Cooking time: 40 mins

1 cup uncooked *rajma* (kidney
    beans; soak for 6–8 hours)
1 cup uncooked rice (soak for
    20 minutes)
1 cup fresh corn (from cob) or
    sweet corn kernels
1 large capsicum, chopped finely
4 small bulbs of spring onion,
    sliced into rings
⅓ cup greens of spring onion,
    chopped finely
2 medium tomatoes
1 large onion, chopped finely
½ tsp red chilli powder
2–3 garlic cloves, chopped finely
2 dry red chillies, broken
9 tbsp readymade salsa
9 tbsp Sour Cream
    (recipe on page 109)
Salt as per taste
2 tbsp oil

1   Cook the rice in boiling water. Strain and spread on a plate
to cool.
2   Pressure-cook the *rajma* with 3 cups of water, dry red chillies,
garlic and 1 tsp salt for 5–6 whistles.
3   Pressure-cook the corn for 5–6 whistles. Strain and set aside.
4   Blanch the tomatoes in boiling water for 5 minutes. Strain and
cool. Peel the skins; chop finely.
5   Heat 1 tbsp oil. Sauté onions for 2 minutes. Add the chili
powder, ½ tsp salt and tomatoes. Sauté for 7–8 minutes, until
mixture starts leaving the sides of the pan.
6   Add cooked *rajma*, along with the water it was cooked in, to the
onion mixture. Cook for 3 minutes; add salt as per taste and
water as required to achieve desired consistency. Keep aside.
7   Heat 1 tbsp oil in another pan and sauté the capsicum for
1 minute. Add ½ tsp salt and sauté for another minute.
8   Add the sliced spring onions; sauté for 1 minute.
9   Add the spring onion greens along with the corn; sauté for
2 minutes.
10 Add the cooked rice and mix well. Add salt as per taste.
11 To serve (for one person), place 1 cup rice in a bowl and
pour ¾ cup *rajma* over it. Top with 1½ tbsp Sour Cream (recipe
on page 109) and then 1½ tbsp salsa.

VALUE PER SERVING		
	Calories	310 kcal
	Protein	11 gms
	Fat	6 gms
	Carbs	33 gms
	Calcium	109 mgs
	Fibre	3 gms
	Iron	3 mgs

• **Gluten-free**

Complete your plate: With a glass of Spicy Buttermilk (recipe on page 153).

GARDEN VEGETABLES with TOFU

Simple to whip up, this gravy dish can easily
become a weekly staple in any household

Makes: 5 cups	Preparation time: 10 mins
Serving size: 1 cup	Cooking time: 25 mins
Serves: 5	

1   Heat water in a large pan. When it comes to the boil,
add broccoli.

2   After 2 minutes, add bell peppers.

3   After another 2 minutes, add mushrooms.

4   Boil for 2 more minutes, then drain.

5   In a separate pan, heat oil; sauté onions until translucent.
Stir in the boiled vegetables. Season with salt and chilli
powder; stir-fry briefly.

6   Mix in the tomatoes; cook for 2 minutes, then add ketchup
and add ½–¾ cup of water. Simmer for about 5 minutes.

7   Add the tofu and cook for another 3–4 minutes. Serve hot.

• Gluten-free

⌛ Quick & Easy

Complete your plate: With steamed rice/noodles and a bowl of curd.

100 gms mushrooms,
   chopped coarsely
200 gms tofu, cubed
1 small head of broccoli (60 gms),
   separated into small florets
2 medium red and yellow bell
   peppers, cubed
2 medium onions, cubed
2 medium tomatoes, cubed
8 tbsp ketchup
1 tsp red chilli powder
Salt as per taste
1 tbsp oil

VALUE PER SERVING		
	Calories	132 kcal
	Protein	8 gms
	Fat	5 gms
	Carbs	15 gms
	Calcium	158 mgs
	Fibre	2 gms
	Iron	0.8 mg

GUILT-FREE HAKKA NOODLES

Indian-style Chinese noodles that won't leave
a coating of grease on your plate or your palate

Makes: 6 cups
Serving size: 1 cup
Serves: 6

Pre-preparation time: 18–20 hrs
Preparation time: 10 mins
Cooking time: 20 mins

2 cup boiled noodles (100 gms uncooked)
1½ cups cabbage, shredded
1 cup carrots, julienned
1 cup French beans, sliced diagonally
4 spring onion bulbs, sliced
¾ cup *moong* sprouts or ¼ cup uncooked green *moong* (soak for 6–8 hours, drain and keep covered for another 12 hours)
150 gms silken tofu, cut into thin long strips
4 green chillies, chopped finely
4 garlic cloves, chopped finely
4 tsp vinegar
1 tsp soy sauce
3 tbsp readymade hot and sweet sauce
2 tbsp oil
Salt as per taste

1 Boil water in a pan and add the *moong* sprouts, carrots and French beans. Cook for 8 minutes. Drain and and set aside.

2 Heat the oil in a pan; sauté garlic and green chillies for 1 minute.

3 Add the spring onions and cabbage with ½ tsp salt; sauté for 2–3 minutes.

4 Mix in the boiled carrots, French beans, sprouts and noodles. Add vinegar, soy sauce, and hot and sweet sauce.

5 Add silken tofu and salt as per taste; mix well. Serve hot.

⧗ **Quick & Easy**

Complete your plate: With a bowl of soup.

VALUE PER SERVING		
Calories	174 kcal
Protein	7 gms
Fat	6 gms
Carbs	23 gms
Calcium	90 mgs
Fibre	1.4 gms
Iron	2.8 mgs

VEGETABLE FRIED RICE

Vegetable fried rice gets a boost with
your choice of egg whites or tofu

Makes: 6 cups
Serving size: 2 cups
Serves: 3

Preparation time: 10 mins
Cooking time: 20 mins

¾ cup uncooked rice
150 gms silken tofu or 6 eggs
1 large onion, chopped finely
½ cup carrots, julienned
½ cup French beans, julienned
½ cup cabbage, julienned
½ cup fresh corn (from cob) or
    sweet corn kernels
4 garlic cloves, chopped finely
1½ tbsp readymade
    red chilli sauce
1 tsp soya sauce
1 tsp vinegar
Salt as per taste
1½ tbsp oil

1   Cook the rice in boiling water. Drain and cool.
2   If using eggs, hard-boil them, remove the shells, slice each
    into half, and scoop out and discard the yolk. Chop the
    egg whites into tiny cubes.
3   If using tofu, cut into tiny cubes.
4   Pressure-cook the corn for 5–6 whistles. Drain and set aside.
5   Heat oil and sauté garlic. Add onions; sauté for 1 minute.
6   Add French beans and salt; sauté for 2 minutes.
7   Add carrots; sauté for another 2 minutes.
8   Add cabbage; sauté for 2 minutes.
9   Add corn and tofu/eggs.
10 Stir in the cooked rice, soya sauce, vinegar, red chilli sauce
    and salt. Cook for another 2 minutes. Serve hot.

• Gluten-free
⧖ Quick & Easy

VALUE PER SERVING		
Calories	265 kcal
Protein	8 gms
Fat	8 gms
Carbs	21 gms
Calcium	46 mgs
Fibre	1 gm
Iron	2 mgs

Complete your plate: With a glass of Spicy Buttermilk (recipe on page 153).

SAUTÉED VEGGIES

A buttery combination of bell peppers, broccoli, baby corn
and tofu/*paneer*, with a bit of salsa for added kick

Makes: 8 cups
Serving size: 2 cups
Serves: 4

Preparation time: 10 mins
Cooking time: 15 mins

1 large red bell pepper, cubed
1 large yellow bell pepper, cubed
1 small head broccoli (60 gms)
12 baby corns
2 packets mushrooms (400 gms)
2 large onions, cubed
200 gms tofu, or *paneer* made
    from 2 litres fat-free milk
    (0–0.8% fat), cubed
4 tbsp readymade salsa
1 tsp oregano
1 tsp black pepper powder
3 tbsp butter
Salt as per taste

1 Rinse the mushrooms in a strainer. Chop each mushroom
   into 4 parts.
2 Chop the baby corn vertically into two halves and then
   horizontally into 3 parts each.
3 Cut the stems of the broccoli and divide into medium-sized
   florets.
4 Rinse the remaining vegetables in a strainer.
5 Heat butter. Sauté the mushrooms, baby corn and broccoli
   with 1 tsp salt for 5 minutes.
6 Add bell peppers and onion with ½ tsp salt; sauté for
   5 minutes.
7 Add tofu or *paneer*, black pepper powder and salt as per taste.
   Cook for 2 minutes.
8 Stir in oregano and salsa and cook for 1 minute. Serve hot.

VALUE PER SERVING		
	Calories	235 kcal
	Protein	14 gms
	Fat	10 gms
	Carbs	19 gms
	Calcium	224 mgs
	Fibre	4 gms
	Iron	2 mgs

• Gluten-free
⧗ Quick & Easy

Complete your plate: With a bowl of Spinach Soup (recipe on page 76).

SPINACH SOUP

A soothing soup of spinach and carrots
flavoured with caramelised onion

FIBRE

Makes: 7 cups
Serving size: 1 cup
Serves: 7

Preparation time: 5 mins
Cooking time: 15 mins

2 bundles spinach (approximately
    250 gms after cleaning)
1 large tomato, quartered
2 medium carrots, peeled
    and sliced
1 small onion, quartered
1 small onion, chopped finely
2 tsp corn flour
2 lemons, quartered and deseeded
Salt as per taste
Black pepper powder as per taste
2 tsp butter

1   Discard the stems of the spinach and rinse the leaves. Drain.
2   Place the spinach leaves, tomatoes, carrot and quartered
    onion in a pan. Add 6 cups of water and 1 tsp salt; cover and
    cook for 10–12 minutes.
3   Once cooled, purée with a hand blender. Pass through a sieve
    and set aside.
4   Heat butter and sauté the chopped onion until golden brown.
    Add corn flour; sauté for another minute.
5   Add the spinach purée.
6   Season with salt and pepper, bring to the boil and cook for
    5–7 minutes.
7   Serve hot with a lemon wedge.

• Gluten-free
⧗ Quick & Easy

VALUE PER SERVING		
Calories	37 kcal
Protein	1 gm
Fat	1 gm
Carbs	5 gms
Calcium	53 mgs
Fibre	0 gm
Iron	1 mg

GARLIC BREAD

Garlic bread gets a burst of spice with
paprika – perfect to add zest to any meal

Makes: 20 slices	**Preparation time: 5 mins**
Serving size: 2 slices	**Cooking time: 20 mins**
Serves: 10	

1 Preheat the oven at 160°C for 7–10 minutes.
2 In a small bowl, mix all the ingredients together.
3 Spread on the bread slices and bake in preheated oven
   for 10 minutes. Serve hot.

⧗ **Quick & Easy**

1 French baguette,
  cut into 20 slices
10 tsp butter, melted
10 garlic cloves, crushed
5 tsp red chilli flakes
Salt as per taste

VALUE PER SERVING		
	Calories	116 kcal
	Protein	2 gms
	Fat	4 gms
	Carbs	17 gms
	Calcium	3 mgs
	Fibre	0 gm
	Iron	0 mg

MUSHROOM and TOFU SOUP

Puréed mushroom and onion soup with diced tofu,
seasoned with a hint of nutmeg and pepper

Makes: 5 cups
Serving size: 1 cup
Serves: 5

Preparation time: 5 mins
Cooking time: 25 mins

150 gms mushrooms,
   chopped coarsely
150 gms silken tofu, diced finely
1 medium onion, chopped coarsely
2 garlic cloves, chopped finely
2 tsp corn flour
½ cup double toned milk
   (1.5% fat)
2 bay leaves
½ tsp black pepper powder
2 pinches of nutmeg powder
5 lemon wedges
Salt as per taste
1 tbsp butter

1 Heat butter. Add garlic and bay leaves; sauté for half a minute.
2 Add onions; sauté until they become translucent.
3 Add mushrooms and ½ tsp salt. Cook for 5 minutes.
4 Pour in 2 cups of water. Bring to the boil and cook for
    5 minutes.
5 Remove from heat and allow cooling, transferring to a flat pan
    to speed up the process.
6 Discard the bay leaves and pour contents of pan into a bowl.
    Grind with a hand blender until smooth.
7 Add milk and return to heat, boiling for 5 minutes.
8 Mix corn flour in ¼ cup water and add to the boiling soup,
    stirring continuously for 2 minutes.
9 Finally, add the tofu cubes, salt, pepper and nutmeg powder;
    cook for 5 minutes.
10 Serve hot with a lemon wedge.

VALUE PER SERVING		
	Calories	73 kcal
	Protein	4 gms
	Fat	4 gms
	Carbs	6 gms
	Calcium	34 mgs
	Fibre	0 gm
	Iron	1 mg

• Gluten-free
⏳ Quick & Easy

Complete your plate: With Garlic Bread (recipe on page 77).

BAKED BEAN and TOMATO SOUP

Baked beans, capsicum and spaghetti in a rich,
sauce-like tomato soup

Makes: 7½ cups	Preparation time: 5 mins
Serving size: 1½ cups	Cooking time: 25 mins
Serves: 5	

1 Blanch the tomatoes. Cool and blend in a liquidiser.
   Sieve and keep aside.
2 Blend baked beans coarsely with ½ cup of water.
3 Heat oil in a pan; sauté onion and capsicum with ½ tsp
   of salt for 5 minutes.
4 Add chilli flakes; sauté for another minute.
5 Combine the tomato purée and bring it to the boil.
6 Add the blended beans along with 1½ cups of water.
7 Bring the mixture to the boil and allow it to simmer for
   about 5 minutes.
8 Add salt, pepper and boiled spaghetti.
9 Garnish with oregano; serve hot.

✻ **Jain**: Omit onions.
⧖ **Quick & Easy**

Complete your plate: With Tricolor Salad (recipe on page 82).

1 can (400 gms) baked beans
1 small onion, chopped finely
1 small capsicum, chopped finely
½ cup cooked spaghetti
   (50 gms uncooked)
5 medium tomatoes
1 tbsp olive oil or any
   other cooking oil
1 tsp red chilli flakes
½ tsp oregano, dried
½ tsp black pepper powder
Salt as per taste

VALUE PER SERVING		
	Calories	145 kcal
	Protein	6 gms
	Fat	3 gms
	Carbs	22 gms
	Calcium	37 mgs
	Fibre	4 gms
	Iron	1 mg

TRICOLOUR SALAD

Baby corn, mushroom and red, yellow and green bell peppers drizzled with an herbed yogurt dressing

Makes: 5 cups
Serving size: 1 cup
Serves: 5

Preparation time: 5 mins
Cooking time: 25 mins

1 Tie the curd in a white muslin cloth and hang for 15 minutes to remove excess water.

2 In a saucepan, bring 2 cups of water to the boil and add sliced baby corn; cook for about 3 minutes. Add bell peppers and continue to boil for 2–3 minutes. Drain.

3 In a separate pan, bring 2 cups of water to boil and add chopped mushrooms. Remove from heat immediately, but drain after 2 minutes.

4 Combine all the boiled vegetables in a salad bowl. Bring them down to room temperature.

5 For the dressing, mix the hung curd with the rest of the ingredients.

6 Toss the veggies with the dressing just before serving.

• Gluten-free
⏳ Quick & Easy

Salad
10 baby corns, sliced
200 gms mushrooms, quartered
1 large red bell pepper, cubed
1 large yellow bell pepper, cubed
1 large capsicum, cubed

Dressing
3 cups thick fresh curd (made from 1.5% fat double-toned milk)
2 tsp green chilli, chopped finely
1 tsp mustard powder
1 tsp black pepper powder
3 tsp powdered sugar
1 tsp black salt
2 tbsp parsley or celery, chopped finely

VALUE PER SERVING		
Calories	122 kcal
Protein	9 gms
Fat	3 gms
Carbs	25 gms
Calcium	178 mgs
Fibre	1 gm
Iron	2 mgs

ONION and PALAK PARATHA

Seasoned with nothing but green chilli, this *paratha* lets the spinach and the onion speak for themselves

Makes: 6 *parathas*
Serving size: 1 *paratha*
Serves: 6

Preparation time: 5 mins
Cooking time: 25 mins

1 cup whole-wheat flour
1 medium onion, chopped finely
½ cup spinach, chopped finely
2 green chillies, chopped finely
1 tsp oil (for the dough)
3 tsp oil (for roasting *parathas*)
Salt as per taste

1 Toss chopped onion with a pinch of salt; set aside for 5 minutes.

2 Sprinkle a pinch of salt over the chopped spinach and mix well; keep aside for 10 minutes.

3 Squeeze out excess water from the spinach.

4 Prepare the dough by kneading together flour, onions, spinach, green chillies, salt, oil and water. Add water as needed to form a soft cohesive ball.

5 Divide the dough into 6 equal parts, using each for one *paratha*. Roll out *parathas* roughly 5-inch in diameter; roast on a non-stick pan using ½ tsp oil for each. Serve hot.

VALUE PER SERVING		
Calories	88 kcal
Protein	2 gms
Fat	3 gms
Carbs	13 gms
Calcium	68 mgs
Fibre	1 gm
Iron	1 mg

⧗ **Quick & Easy**

CHOLE PALAK

A leaner, meaner version of *chole*,
loaded with spinach

Makes: 7 cups	Pre-preparation time: 6–8 hrs	
Serving size: 1 cup	Preparation time: 10 mins	
Serves: 7	Cooking time: 35 mins	

1 Pressure-cook chickpeas with 1 tsp salt and 4 cups water for 8–10 whistles.
2 Clean the spinach thoroughly, discard the stems and chop coarsely.
3 Place spinach leaves, tomatoes, and 1 tsp of salt in a pan. Cover and cook for 10 minutes (do not add water). Allow to cool, then separate the spinach and tomatoes.
4 In a blender, grind the tomatoes and green chillies to a paste.
5 Separately grind spinach leaves (not a smooth paste).
6 Heat oil in a pan; sauté garlic. Add onions; sauté until browned. Add the tomato paste and cook for 5–7 minutes.
7 Season with *jeera* powder and red chilli powder.
8 Cook till the paste leaves the sides of the pan, then add spinach purée and cook for a few more minutes.
9 Add the boiled chickpeas and salt; cook for 2 minutes. Serve hot.

• **Gluten-free**

Complete your plate: With Onion and *Palak Parathas* (recipe on page 83) and a bowl of curd.

4 bundles spinach (500–600 gms after cleaning)
1 cup uncooked chickpeas (soak for 6–8 hours)
2 large tomatoes, quartered
2 medium onions, chopped finely
5–6 garlic cloves, chopped finely
3–4 green chillies
1 tsp red chilli powder
1½ tsp *jeera* powder (cumin powder)
2 tsp oil
Salt as per taste

VALUE PER SERVING		
Calories	148 kcal
Protein	6 gms
Fat	5 gms
Carbs	19 gms
Calcium	134 mgs
Fibre	2 gms
Iron	2 mgs

BLACK DAL

A mildly seasoned North Indian staple
that's high in protein and big on taste

Makes: 8 cups	Pre-preparation time: 6–8 hrs
Serving size: 1 cup	Preparation time: 10 mins
Serves: 8	Cooking time: 30 mins

1½ cups uncooked whole *urad*
(black gram; soak for
6–8 hours)
½ cup uncooked *rajma* (kidney
beans; soak for 6–8 hours)
4 medium tomatoes
2-inch piece of ginger, julienned
7–8 garlic cloves, chopped finely
2 dry red chillies
3½ tsp red chilli powder
4–5 bay leaves
3 tbsp oil
Salt as per taste

1 Drain the soaked *rajma* and *urad*; rinse thoroughly (make
   sure you discard the water in which it is soaked, for health
   purposes).
2 Pressure-cook the mixture with 6 cups of water, 2 tsp salt
   and the dry red chillies. Cook for 4–5 whistles.
3 In the meantime, chop each tomato into 4 pieces and grind
   in mixer. Sieve the purée and set aside.
4 Heat oil in a pan and fry the bay leaves for a few seconds.
   Add ginger and garlic; sauté for half a minute and then add
   red chilli powder.
5 Immediately add the tomato purée; cook for 5 minutes.
   Add *urad* and *rajma* mixture.
6 Depending on the consistency you desire, add 1–2 cups
   of water.
7 Pressure-cook again for 1 whistle, then reduce to a low flame
   and cook for another 10 minutes.
8 Remove from heat; open lid once pressure has been released.
   Adjust consistency.
9 Serve piping hot.

VALUE PER SERVING		
	Calories	186 kcal
	Protein	9.5 gms
	Fat	5 gms
	Carbs	25 gms
	Calcium	88 mgs
	Fibre	1.4 gms
	Iron	2 mgs

✶ **Jain**: Replace ginger and garlic with ½ tsp *garam masala*.
● **Gluten-free**

Complete your plate: With steamed rice and Quick Cabbage Salad (recipe
on page 88).

QUICK CABBAGE SALAD

Cabbage, potatoes and spring onion
tossed in salad oil and seasoning

Makes: 6 cups
Serving size: ¾ cup
Serves: 8

Preparation time: 5 mins
Cooking time: 5 mins

4 cups cabbage, julienned
2 small potatoes, boiled,
   peeled and diced
4 tbsp greens of spring onion,
   chopped coarsely
4 tbsp peanuts, roasted and
   ground coarsely
3–4 tsp lime juice
1 tsp red chilli flakes
Salt as per taste
2 tsp salad oil or olive oil

1   Toss together all the ingredients to make a salad.
2   Serve immediately or chilled.

• Gluten-free
⌛ Quick & Easy

VALUE PER SERVING		
Calories	62 kcal
Protein	2.5 gms
Fat	3.3 gms
Carbs	6 gms
Calcium	30 mgs
Fibre	0.6 gm
Iron	0.5 mg

BASIC WRAP

Have this with any of our filling
recipes or one of your own

Makes: 12 wraps

1 Combine wheat flour, *maida*, water and 1 tsp oil; knead into
   a soft dough.
2 Divide into 12 equal parts.
3 Roll out wraps (each wrap should measure 6 inches in diameter).
4 Heat a *tawa* and roast the wraps on both sides using ½ tsp oil
   for each wrap.

1 cup whole-wheat flour
1 cup *maida* (all-purpose flour)
¾ cup water
1 tsp oil (to add to dough)
6 tsp oil (for roasting the wraps)

CORN and TOFU ROLL

A tangy mix of fresh corn, tofu, capsicum
and onion held together with potato

Makes: 10 rolls
Serving size: 2 rolls
Serves: 5

Preparation time: 25 mins
Cooking time: 10 mins

1 cup fresh corn (from cob) or
   sweet corn kernels, boiled
200 gms tofu, diced
2 medium onions, chopped finely
2 large capsicum, chopped finely
2 large potatoes, boiled and diced
2 green chillies, chopped finely
3 tbsp fresh coriander,
   chopped finely
2 tsp *chaat masala*
1 tsp *amchur* powder
   (dry mango powder)
Salt as per taste
1½ tbsp oil
10 basic wraps (recipe on page 89)

1   Heat oil in a pan and add onions, green chillies and capsicum;
     sauté for about 2 minutes.

2   Add the potato, corn, *chaat masala*, *amchur* powder and salt.

3   Mix in tofu and fresh coriander. Remove from heat.
     Use ⅓ cup grated cheese to enhance the taste (optional).

4   Place ⅓ cup of the mixture on each basic wrap and make
     a roll.

⏳ Quick & Easy

Complete your plate: With a glass of Spicy Buttermilk (recipe on page 153).

VALUE PER SERVING		
	Calories	325 kcal
	Protein	12 gms
	Fat	8.8 gms
	Carbs	49 gms
	Calcium	218 mgs
	Fibre	3 gms
	Iron	2 mgs

MOONG and VEGETABLE ROLL

French beans, carrots and sprouts spiced up
with a mouth-watering blend of *masala*

Makes: 12 rolls
Serving size: 2 rolls
Serves: 6

Pre-preparation: 18–20 hrs
Preparation time: 25 mins
Cooking time: 15 mins

2 cups *moong* sprouts or ¾ cup
   uncooked green *moong* (soak
   for 6–8 hours, drain and keep
   covered for another 12 hours)
1 cup carrots, chopped finely
1 cup French beans, chopped finely
2 medium onions, chopped finely
3 green chillies, chopped finely
1-inch piece of ginger, grated
3 tbsp fresh coriander,
   chopped finely
¼ tsp turmeric powder
2 tsp coriander powder
1 tsp *jeera* powder (cumin powder)
1 tsp red chilli powder
½ tsp *amchur* powder
   (dry mango powder)
Salt as per taste
2 tbsp oil
12 basic wraps (recipe on page 89)

1 Pressure-cook the *moong* with ½ tsp of salt for 1 whistle.
   Manually diffuse the pressure by letting the steam out and
   open immediately. Drain and set aside.

2 Pressure-cook the carrots and beans with 2 cups of water
   for 1 whistle. Cool, drain and set aside.

3 Heat the oil in a saucepan; sauté the onions for 1 minute.
   Add ginger, green chillies and turmeric powder; sauté for
   half a minute.

4 Add *moong* and the cooked vegetables with the remaining
   seasonings. Cook until water dries up. Stir in fresh coriander.

5 Place ⅓ cup mixture on each basic wrap and make a roll.

⌛ Quick & Easy

Complete your plate: With a glass of Spicy Buttermilk (recipe on page 153).

VALUE PER SERVING		
	Calories	284 kcal
	Protein	12 gms
	Fat	4 gms
	Carbs	50 gms
	Calcium	135 mgs
	Fibre	2.4 gms
	Iron	3.3 mgs

CHOLE and PALAK ROLL

A filling of *chole* combined with the goodness of spinach

Makes: 10 rolls
Serving size: 2 rolls
Serves: 5

Pre-preparation time: 6–8 hrs
Preparation time: 25 mins
Cooking time: 15 mins

1 cup uncooked chickpeas
   (soak for 6–8 hours)
1 cup spinach, chopped finely
2 medium onions, chopped finely
2 medium tomatoes,
   chopped finely
3 green chillies, chopped finely
2-inch piece of ginger, julienned
4 garlic cloves, grated
3 tsp *chole masala*
1 tsp *amchur* powder
   (dry mango powder)
1½ tsp red chilli powder
1 tbsp oil
Salt as per taste
10 basic wraps (recipe on page 89)

1 Drain and rinse chickpeas; pressure-cook with 4 cups of water 1 tsp of salt for 7 whistles. Drain.

2 Heat oil in a pan and sauté onions until light brown, for about 5 minutes.

3 Add garlic, ginger and green chillies; sauté for 1 minute.

4 Add tomatoes and ½ tsp of salt; sauté for another minute.

5 Add spinach and cook for about 4 minutes.

6 Add *chole masala*, *amchur* and chilli powder and mix well; sauté for 1 minute.

7 Add boiled chickpeas; cook till *masala* coats the chickpeas, approximately 1 minute.

8 Place ⅓ cup of the mixture on each basic wrap and make a roll.

✻ **Jain**: Omit onion, garlic and ginger.
⧖ **Quick & Easy**

Complete your plate: With a glass of Spicy Buttermilk (recipe on page 153).

VALUE PER SERVING		
	Calories	313 kcal
	Protein	11 gms
	Fat	8 gms
	Carbs	49 gms
	Calcium	229 mgs
	Fibre	3 gms
	Iron	4 mgs

RAJMA ROLL

A mildly spiced filling of kidney beans
and capsicum in a tomato base

Makes: 12 rolls
Serving size: 2 rolls
Serves: 6

Pre-preparation time: 6–8 hrs
Preparation time: 25 mins
Cooking time: 30 mins

1 cup uncooked *rajma* (kidney
   beans; soak for 6–8 hours)
2 medium onions, chopped finely
1 large capsicum, chopped finely
2 medium tomatoes,
   chopped finely
½ tsp black pepper powder
3 tsp red chilli powder
2 tbsp ketchup
1 tbsp oil
Salt as per taste
12 basic wraps (recipe on page 89)

1   Drain and rinse kidney beans; pressure-cook for 8 whistles
    with 3 cups of water.
2   Heat oil in a pan; sauté onions and capsicum with 1 tsp salt
    for 4 minutes.
3   Add red chilli powder; sauté for 5 seconds. Add tomatoes;
    sauté for 10 minutes. Then add ketchup, salt and pepper.
4   Add the beans and cook for 2–3 minutes or till water dries up.
5   Place ⅓ cup of the mixture on each basic wrap and make
    a roll.

✻ **Jain**: Replace onions with finely chopped cabbage.
⌛ **Quick & Easy**

Complete your plate: With a glass of Spicy Buttermilk (recipe on page 153).

VALUE PER SERVING		
	Calories	282 kcal
	Protein	11 gms
	Fat	6 gms
	Carbs	47 gms
	Calcium	103 mgs
	Fibre	1.5 gms
	Iron	3 mgs

TOFU PALAK ROLL

Fresh greens and tofu flavoured
with onion, *jeera* and pepper

Makes: 10 rolls
Serving size: 2 rolls
Serves: 5

Preparation time: 25 mins
Cooking time: 10 mins

100 gms tofu, grated coarsely
  or diced
1½ cups spinach, chopped finely
1½ cups cabbage, shredded
2 medium onions, chopped finely
4 green chillies, chopped finely
1 tsp *jeera* powder (cumin powder)
½ tsp black pepper powder
1½ tbsp ketchup
Salt as per taste
2 tbsp oil
10 basic wraps (recipe on page 89)

1 Heat oil in a pan; sauté chopped onion and green chillies
  for 1 minute.
2 Add cumin powder; sauté for 1 minute.
3 Add spinach; sauté for 2 minutes.
4 Add cabbage; sauté for 2 minutes.
5 Add tofu, salt and pepper; sauté for 1 minute.
6 Remove from heat and add ketchup. Mix well.
7 Place ⅓ cup of the mixture on each basic wrap and
  make a roll.

✳ **Jain**: Omit onions.
⧗ **Quick & Easy**

Complete your plate: With a glass of Spicy Buttermilk (recipe on page 153).

VALUE PER SERVING		
	Calories	245 kcal
	Protein	8 gms
	Fat	9 gms
	Carbs	33 gms
	Calcium	166 mgs
	Fibre	1 gm
	Iron	2 mgs

BOMBAY BHAJI ROLL

The irresistible taste of *pav bhaji* wrapped in whole-wheat goodness… this mixed vegetable wrap is a quick fix

Makes: 8 rolls
Serving size: 2 rolls
Serves: 4

Preparation time: 25 mins
Cooking time: 25 mins

2 cups green peas
4 medium tomatoes, chopped finely
2 large capsicum, chopped finely
100 gms tofu/*paneer*, grated coarsely
4 tsp *pav bhaji masala*
1 tsp red chilli powder
1 tbsp oil
Salt as per taste
8 basic wraps (recipe on page 89)

1 Pressure-cook peas for 2 whistles. Drain, cool and mash lightly.
2 Heat oil in a pan; sauté capsicum for 2 minutes.
3 Add tomatoes; sauté for 10 minutes or until all the water dries up.
4 Add *pav bhaji masala* and stir-fry briefly.
5 Add grated tofu, mashed peas, salt and red chilli powder. Cook on low heat until almost dry.
6 Place ⅓ cup of the mixture on each basic wrap and make a roll. Cut each wrap into 3–4 pieces and serve.

❋ **Jain**
⧖ **Quick & Easy**

Complete your plate: With a glass of Spicy Buttermilk (recipe on page 153).

VALUE PER SERVING		
Calories	315 kcal
Protein	13 gms
Fat	9 gms
Carbs	44 gms
Calcium	198 mgs
Fibre	5 gms
Iron	3 mgs

DOUBLE-SIDED EGG ROLL

A nutritious take on *baida roti* with whole-wheat *rotis* encased in egg and stuffed with a flavourful cabbage filling

Makes: 6 rolls
Serving size: 2 rolls
Serves: 3

Preparation time: 5 mins
Cooking time: 20 mins

12 egg whites
4 cups cabbage, julienned
2 large onions, sliced
2 green chillies, chopped finely
2 tbsp fresh coriander, chopped finely
½ tsp turmeric powder
2½ tbsp oil
Salt as per taste
6 basic wraps (recipe on page 89)

1 Heat 1½ tbsp oil. Add green chillies and turmeric powder.
2 Immediately add onions; sauté for 1 minute.
3 Add cabbage; sauté for 2 minutes.
4 Add salt; sauté for another 2 minutes.
5 Add the coriander and keep aside.
6 Heat a non-stick pan and drizzle with ½ tsp oil.
7 Pour 1 egg white (beaten with a pinch of salt) into the pan; immediately place one basic wrap over it.
8 Cook on a slow flame for 1 minute.
9 Add another beaten egg white over the wrap.
10 Carefully turn it over and cook for 2 minutes.
11 Place the wrap on a foil.
12 Put ⅓ cup of the cabbage mixture on each wrap and make a roll. Wrap the roll in foil. Repeat for remaining 5 rolls.

VALUE PER SERVING		
Calories	330 kcal
Protein	18.5 gms
Fat	10.5 gms
Carbs	37 gms
Calcium	141 mgs
Fibre	2.5 gms
Iron	1.6 mgs

⧗ **Quick & Easy**

Complete your plate: With a glass of Spicy Buttermilk (recipe on page 153).

ALOO MATAR TOFU ROLL

A wrap with a spicy filling of potato, peas and
tofu – the perfect fix for a burger craving

Makes: 12 rolls	**Preparation time:** 25 mins
Serving size: 2 rolls	**Cooking time:** 10 mins
Serves: 6	

1 Pressure-cook the peas with 2 cups water for 1 whistle.
   Drain and keep aside.

2 Heat oil in a pan. Add *jeera*; when it begins to change colour,
   add green chillies and sauté for 5 seconds.

3 Add the boiled peas and season with turmeric powder,
   red chilli powder, coriander powder and salt; sauté for
   1–2 minutes.

4 Add potato, tofu, *garam masala*, *chaat masala*, *amchur*
   powder, *jeera* powder, fresh coriander and sugar; sauté
   for 2 minutes, then remove from heat.

5. Place ⅓ cup mixture on each basic wrap and make a roll.

✣ **Jain:** Replace potatoes with 1 cup cauliflower (separated into florets
   and boiled).

⏳ **Quick & Easy**

Complete your plate: With a bowl of curd.

100 gms tofu, diced
1 cup green peas
2 medium potatoes, boiled
   and diced
2 tbsp fresh coriander,
   chopped finely
2–3 green chillies, chopped finely
1 tsp *jeera* (cumin seeds)
½ tsp turmeric powder
2 tsp red chilli powder
2 tsp coriander powder
1 tsp *jeera* powder (cumin powder)
1 tsp *amchur* powder
   (dry mango powder)
1 tsp *chaat masala*
2 pinches *garam masala*
1 tsp powdered sugar
4 tsp oil
Salt as per taste
12 basic wraps (recipe on page 89)

VALUE PER SERVING		
Calories	260 kcal
Protein	9 gms
Fat	7 gms
Carbs	40 gms
Calcium	148 mgs
Fibre	2.6 gms
Iron	3 mgs

CHOLE TIKKI

Soft-centred vegetable cutlets crisped on the
outside, topped with spicy chickpea gravy

Makes: 6 cups *chole* and 12 *tikkis*
Serving size: 1 cup *chole* with
        2 *tikkis*
Serves: 6

Pre-preparation time: 6–8 hrs
Preparation time: 30 mins
Cooking time: 35 mins

Chole

1 cup uncooked chickpeas
    (soak for 6–8 hours)
1 large onion, chopped coarsely
3 green chillies, slit
2-inch piece of ginger, julienned
¼ cup tamarind
2 tsp *chole masala*
2 tsp coriander powder
½ tsp *jeera* powder
    (cumin powder)
¼ tsp *garam masala*
2–3 bay leaves
2 tbsp oil
Salt as per taste

Tikkis

2 slices brown or white bread (4"× 4")
4 cups cauliflower (approximately
    300 gms after discarding stems
    and dividing into small florets)
2 medium potatoes, boiled
2 tsp oil
Salt as per taste

Chole

1 Drain and rinse chickpeas; pressure-cook with 1 tsp salt and
   5 cups of water for 8–10 whistles. Drain; reserve the water.
2 Soak tamarind in ½ cup water for 30 minutes. After it
   becomes soft, sieve through a strainer and reserve water.
   This is the tamarind water.
3 In a mixer, grind onions and green chillies.
4 In a large saucepan, heat 2 tbsp oil; toss in bay leaves and
   ginger. Add the onion paste and sauté for 15 minutes or
   until brown. Add coriander powder and *chole masala* and
   sauté for another 2 minutes.
5 Mix in the boiled chickpeas along with water.
6 Add *garam masala*, *jeera* powder, tamarind water and salt.
   If required, add water to achieve desired consistency.
   Cook for 3–4 minutes.

Tikkis

1 Boil cauliflower in water until tender. Drain and squeeze
   out all the excess water. Mash along with boiled potatoes.
2 Grind the bread slices in a mixer. Add to the cauliflower-
   potato mixture along with salt.
3 Divide into 12 portions and make small round *tikkis*. Roast
   on a non-stick pan using 2 tsp oil.
   continued on next page…

VALUE PER SERVING		
	Calories	256 kcal
	Protein	8 gms
	Fat	8 gms
	Carbs	38 gms
	Calcium	94 mgs
	Fibre	2.5 gms
	Iron	3 mgs

CHOLE TIKKI

To serve
1 Spread 1 cup *chole* on two *tikkis* and garnish with fresh coriander.
2 If desired, drizzle with Sweet Chutney (recipe on page 128) and Green Chutney (recipe on page 152).

Complete your plate: With a bowl of Quick Cabbage Salad (recipe on page 88) and a bowl of curd.

LOW-FAT MAYO

A healthier option of the creamy sauce that
will liven up even the dullest dishes

Makes: 1 cup | Preparation time: 1 hr

1   Hang the curd in a muslin cloth for 1 hour.
2   Untie the curd and combine with the remaining ingredients.

2 cups fat-free curd, made
    from 400 ml fat-free milk
    (0–0.8% fat)
½ cup cabbage, julienned
½ tsp *jeera* powder
    (cumin powder)
½ tsp powdered sugar
¼ tsp black pepper powder
Salt as per taste

SOUR CREAM

The perfect homemade creamy dip that
you can be used with chips or veggies

Makes: 1 cup | Preparation time: 1 hr

1   Hang the curd in a muslin cloth for 1 hour.
2   Untie the hung curd and mix it with mayo, cheese spread
    and salt.

2 cups fat-free curd; made
    from 400 ml fat-free milk
    (0–0.8% fat)
1 tbsp readymade low-fat
    mayonnaise
1 tbsp cheese spread
Salt as per taste

SPINACH TOFU PARATHA

A delicate filling of spinach, tofu and potato,
cased in a crisp whole-wheat *paratha*

Makes: 10 *parathas*
Serving size: 2 *parathas*
Serves: 5

Preparation time: 10 mins
Cooking time: 10 mins

2¼ cups whole-wheat flour
1½ cups tofu, crumbled
1½ cups spinach, chopped finely
1 medium potato, boiled
 and grated
2 green chillies, chopped finely
2 tsp *amchur* powder
 (dried mango powder)
1 tsp turmeric powder
Salt as per taste
5 tsp oil (for roasting *parathas*)

1 Sprinkle a pinch of salt over the chopped spinach and mix well;
   keep aside for 10 minutes.
2 Prepare the dough by combining 2 cups of the flour, water
   and some salt; set aside.
3 Squeeze out excess water from the spinach.
4 Combine the spinach, potato, tofu, green chillies, *amchur*
   powder, turmeric powder and salt. Divide this stuffing into
   10 equal parts.
5 Next, divide the dough into 10 equal parts. Roll out one
   part into a *roti* that is 3 inches in diameter. Dust with flour,
   as necessary, to prevent it from sticking to the work surface.
6 Place one part of the stuffing in the centre and fold the edges
   of the *roti* over the stuffing. Pinch the edges together to seal
   the stuffing.
7 Flatten the stuffed *paratha* and roll out again until it is
   5 inches in diameter.
8 Cook the *paratha* on a *tawa* over a medium flame using
   ½ tsp oil till both sides are golden brown.
9 Repeat with the remaining dough and stuffing to make
   9 more *parathas*.
10 Serve hot.

VALUE PER SERVING		
Calories	232 kcal
Protein	8 gms
Fat	6 gms
Carbs	36 gms
Calcium	222 mgs
Fibre	2 gms
Iron	3 mgs

⏳ **Quick & Easy**

Complete your plate: With fresh curd seasoned with red chilli powder,
jeera powder (cumin powder) and salt.

MATAR PANEER PARATHA

Stuffed *paratha* with lip-smackingly spiced
homemade *paneer* and puréed peas

Makes: 13 *parathas*
Serving size: 2 *parathas*
Serves: 6

Preparation time: 10 mins
Cooking time: 25 mins

Dough

2½ cups whole-wheat flour
A pinch of salt
1 tsp oil (to add to dough)
6 tsp oil (for roasting the *parathas*)

Filling

1. Bring milk to the boil and turn off flame. Immediately add lemon juice and stir until milk curdles. Strain through a muslin cloth, making sure all the liquid or whey is removed. What remains in the cloth is *paneer*.
2. Rinse the peas in running water and drain. Place peas, green chillies and ginger in a mixer and grind to a smooth paste, without adding any water.
3. Heat the oil in a pan. Pour in the paste and sauté for 2–3 minutes.
4. Add salt; sauté for 2 more minutes.
5. Add *jeera* powder and *amchur* powder; sauté till the paste leaves the sides of the pan. Remove from heat.
6. Grate the *paneer* and add to the pan. Mix well. Set aside to cool.
7. Divide the filling into 13 parts, rolling each part into a ball. Set aside and prepare the *paratha* dough.

Filling

400 ml fat-free milk (0–0.8% fat)
2 cups green peas
6–8 green chillies, halved
1-inch piece of ginger, julienned
¾ tsp *jeera* powder (cumin powder)
¾ tsp *amchur* powder (dry mango powder)
1 tbsp lemon juice
1 tbsp oil
Salt as per taste

VALUE PER SERVING		
Calories	238 kcal
Protein	9 gms
Fat	7 gms
Carbs	35 gms
Calcium	219 mgs
Fibre	2 gms
Iron	3 mgs

Parathas

1. Combine the wheat flour, a pinch of salt, 1 tsp of oil and water and knead into a soft dough.
2. Divide the dough into 13 equal parts.
3. Roll out 4-inch *rotis* with each part. Place one part of the pea filling in the centre of each *roti*. Fold in all sides over the filling and roll out again.
4. Heat a *tawa* and cook each *paratha* using ½ tsp oil. Roast on both sides until golden brown. Serve hot.

Complete your plate: With a bowl of Hariyali *Raita* (recipe on page 114).

HARIYALI RAITA

Cooked spinach drenched in curd with just
enough spices to complement any dish

Makes: 5 cups
Serving size: ¾ cup
Serves: 6

Preparation time: 5 mins
Cooking time: 10 mins

3 cups fat-free curd, made
    from 600 ml fat-free milk
    (0–0.8% fat)
2 cups spinach, chopped finely
2 small green chillies,
    chopped finely
1-inch piece of ginger, grated
1½ tsp *jeera* powder
    (cumin powder)
1½ tsp rock salt
2 tsp powdered sugar
2 tsp Green Chutney
    (recipe on page 152)
1 cup water
1 tsp mustard seeds
Salt as per taste
2 tsp oil

1 Rinse the spinach and place in a pan.
2 Add ¼ cup water; cover and cook for 5 minutes. Strain
   and set aside to cool.
3 Sieve the curd.
4 Combine spinach, rock salt, salt, cumin powder, sugar,
   green chutney and 1 cup water with the curd. Mix well
   to form the *raita*.
5 Heat oil. Add mustard seeds; once they begin to splutter,
   add green chillies and ginger.
6 Add this to the *raita* and stir well. Serve chilled.

• Gluten-free
⧗ Quick & Easy

VALUE PER SERVING		
	Calories	56 kcal
	Protein	3 gms
	Fat	2 gms
	Carbs	7 gms
	Calcium	142 mgs
	Fibre	0 gm
	Iron	1 mg

MIXED VEGGIE PARATHA

Cabbage, carrot, capsicum and bottle gourd rolled
into a dough simply flavoured with onion seeds

Makes: 9 *parathas*
Serving size: 1 *paratha*
Serves: 9

Preparation time: 10 mins
Cooking time: 10 mins

1 Squeeze out excess water from the grated vegetables.
2 Combine all the ingredients (except 4½ tsp oil) to make
   a dough. Do not add water.
3 Divide the dough into 9 equal portions and roll out 5-inch
   parathas with each portion.
4 Roast the *parathas* on a *tawa* over a medium flame using
   ½ tsp oil, flipping them over to ensure both sides are evenly
   golden brown. Serve hot.

⌛ **Quick & Easy**

¾ cup whole-wheat flour
¾ cup *maida* (all-purpose flour)
¼ cup cabbage, grated
¼ cup carrot, grated
1 small capsicum, chopped finely
¼ cup bottle gourd, grated
¼ cup low-fat curd, made
   from 50 ml double-toned milk
   (1.5% fat)
2 tbsp coriander leaves,
   chopped finely
¼ tsp *kalonji* (onion seeds)
1 tbsp oil
2 tsp salt (or as per taste)
4½ tsp oil (for roasting *parathas*)

VALUE PER SERVING		
Calories	91 kcal
Protein	2 gms
Fat	3 gms
Carbs	13 gms
Calcium	40 mgs
Fibre	0 gm
Iron	1 mg

MASOOR DAL

This wholesome dal is made with red lentils,
with a kick of garlic and red chilli 'tadka'

Makes: 5½ cups
Serving size: 1 cup
Serves: 5

Preparation time: 5 mins
Cooking time: 20 mins

1 cup uncooked *masoor*
   (whole red lentils with skin)
1 large tomato, chopped finely
1 medium onion, chopped finely
4 garlic cloves, chopped finely
5 cups water
½ tsp *jeera* (cumin seeds)
3 green chillies, quartered
   lengthwise
2 dry red chillies, broken
1 tsp red chilli powder
4–5 bay leaves
1½ tbsp oil
1 tsp salt or as per taste

1   Rinse the dal thoroughly; pressure-cook with 3 cups of water
    and 1 tsp salt for 6–7 whistles.
2   Heat oil; add *jeera*. Once seeds begin to splutter, add bay
    leaves, dry red chillies, garlic, green chillies and onion; sauté
    for 2 minutes.
3   Add tomato; sauté for 3–4 minutes.
4   Add red chilli powder and sauté for half a minute.
5   Add the cooked dal and 2 cups water. Simmer to get desired
    consistency. Serve hot.

⧗ **Quick & Easy**

Complete your plate: With Mix Veggie *Paratha* (recipe on page 115) and
a glass of Spicy Buttermilk (recipe on page 153).

VALUE PER SERVING		
	Calories	137 kcal
	Protein	7 gms
	Fat	3 gms
	Carbs	19 gms
	Calcium	37 mgs
	Fibre	1 gm
	Iron	2 mgs

VEGETABLE DAL DALIA

A traditional Gujarati dish known as *Fada Ni Khichdi*, loaded with veggies, broken wheat and dal

Makes: 12 cups
Serving size: 2 cups
Serves: 6

Pre-preparation time: 15 mins
Preparation time: 10 mins
Cooking time: 20 mins

1   Rinse and drain soaked dal; set aside.
2   Heat a pan and roast *dalia*, without adding oil, for 1 minute; set aside.
3   Heat oil; add *jeera*. When the seeds begin to splutter, add bay leaves, ginger, garlic, green chillies and onions; sauté for 1 minute.
4   Add tomato; sauté for another minute.
5   Mix in carrots, French beans, *dudhi*, peas, *garam masala*, red chilli powder, turmeric powder and salt.
6   Transfer to a pressure cooker. Add the soaked dal and roasted *dalia*.
7   Season with salt and add 8 cups of water. Cook for 2 whistles.
8   Let stand until the pressure has been released. Remove the lid and cook for an additional 5 minutes.
9   Garnish with chopped coriander and serve hot.

✻ **Jain**: Omit onion, ginger and garlic; replace carrots with 1 cup shredded cabbage.
⧗ **Quick & Easy**

Complete your plate: With a bowl of curd.

1 cup uncooked yellow or green *moong* dal (soak for 15 minutes)
1 cup *dalia/lapsi* (broken wheat)
2 large onions, chopped coarsely
2 large tomatoes, chopped coarsely
1 cup carrots, chopped coarsely
1 cup French beans, chopped coarsely
1 cup *dudhi* (bottle gourd), chopped coarsely
1 cup fresh green peas
3 green chillies, slit
2-inch stick of ginger, sliced
4–6 garlic cloves, chopped finely
2 tbsp fresh coriander, chopped finely
1 tsp *jeera* (cumin seeds)
2 tsp red chilli powder
½ tsp turmeric powder
½ tsp *garam masala*
4–5 bay leaves
Salt as per taste
3 tbsp oil

VALUE PER SERVING		
Calories	315 kcal
Protein	12 gms
Fat	7 gms
Carbs	50 gms
Calcium	100 mgs
Fibre	3 gms
Iron	4 mgs

TOFU JHALFRAZIE

Fresh veggies and tofu in a thick, Indian-style gravy that packs a punch with its green chilli and *garam masala*

Makes: 8 cups
Serving size: 1½ cups
Serves: 5

Preparation time: 5 mins
Cooking time: 25 mins

1½ cups carrots, chopped coarsely
1½ cups cauliflower, broken into
   small florets
1 cup French beans,
   chopped coarsely
1 cup green peas
100 gms tofu, grated or diced
2 large onions, chopped coarsely
1 large capsicum,
   chopped coarsely
4 large tomatoes,
   chopped coarsely
1½ cups cold fat-free milk
   (0–0.8%)
2 tbsp corn flour
6 green chillies
1 tsp red chilli powder
½ tsp *garam masala*
2 tsp sugar
¼ tsp pepper
Salt as per taste
2 tbsp oil

1   Boil French beans, cauliflower, carrot and green peas in water for 5 minutes. Drain and set aside.
2   Blanch tomatoes in boiling water for 4 minutes; allow to cool, then peel.
3   Purée the peeled tomatoes in a mixer with green chillies.
4   Heat oil in a pan. Add onion; sauté until translucent.
5   Add capsicum and salt; sauté for 1 minute.
6   Next add the boiled veggies, red chilli powder and *garam masala*; sauté for 2 minutes.
7   Stir in the tomato purée, salt, sugar and pepper. Simmer for 5 minutes.
8   In a separate bowl, dissolve corn flour in milk; add this mixture to the pan. Mix well; simmer for another 2–3 minutes.
9   Add tofu and cook for 2 minutes. Serve hot.

• **Gluten-free**
⧗ **Quick & Easy**

Complete your plate: With brown rice and a glass of Spicy Buttermilk (recipe on page 153).

VALUE PER SERVING		
	Calories	236 kcal
	Protein	11.6 gms
	Fat	6 gms
	Carbs	32 gms
	Calcium	250 mgs
	Fibre	4 gms
	Iron	3 mgs

CURD RICE

A cold, South Indian-style dish with
mustard seed and curry leaf 'tadka'

Makes: 5 cups
Serving size: 1½ cups
Serves: 3

Pre-preparation time: 30 mins
Preparation time: 5 mins
Cooking time: 10 mins

1 cup uncooked rice
5 cups low-fat curd, made
   from 1 litre double-toned milk
   (1.5% fat)
2 green chillies, quartered
   lengthwise
1 tsp mustard seeds
7–8 curry leaves
4 dry red chillies, broken into 2
2 tsp powdered sugar
2 tbsp fresh coriander,
   chopped finely
2 tsp oil
2 tsp salt (or as per taste)

1   Hang the curd in a muslin cloth for 30 minutes, allowing the
    excess liquid or whey to drain out. Discard this whey and
    keep the thickened curd aside.
2   Boil the rice until cooked completely. Drain and set aside.
3   Heat oil in a pan; add mustard seeds. When the seeds begin
    to splutter, add green chillies, dry red chillies and curry leaves.
4   Sauté for a few seconds, then remove from heat.
5   Add cooked rice, salt and sugar. Allow to cool completely.
6   Mix in the curd until well blended.
7   Garnish with chopped coriander and serve.

✵ **Jain:** Omit ginger.
● **Gluten-free**
⧗ **Quick & Easy**

Complete your plate: Serve with Chickpea *Chaat* (recipe on page 159).

VALUE PER SERVING		
Calories	214 kcal
Protein	8.5 gms
Fat	3 gms
Carbs	18 gms
Calcium	282 mgs
Fibre	0 gm
Iron	1.5 mgs

USAL

A zesty Maharashtrian dish of sprouted pulses packed with loads of flavour, typically served with *pav*

Makes: 7 cups	Pre-preparation time: 18–20 hrs
Serving size: 1½ cups	Preparation time: 5 mins
Serves: 4–5	Cooking time: 25 mins

1. Pressure-cook the mixed sprouts with 1 tsp salt for 4 whistles with 4 cups water and turmeric powder.
2. Heat 1 tsp oil and add onions; sauté for 5 minutes. Cool.
3. In a separate pan, heat 2 tsp oil. Add *jeera*, dry red *Kashmiri* chillies, green chillies, ginger, garlic, cinnamon, peppercorns and cloves; sauté for 2–3 minutes. Cool.
4. In a blender, grind the cooled sautéed onion, roasted seasonings and coriander powder to a fine paste.
5. Heat 3 tsp oil; sauté the paste for 7–8 minutes.
6. Stir in tomato purée; sauté for 8–10 minutes till it leaves sides of the pan.
7. Add the cooked sprouts along with the water in which they were cooked and add 1 tsp salt. Simmer for about 10 minutes.
8. Garnish with chopped onions and tomatoes before serving. Serve hot with whole-wheat *pav* or steamed rice.

❧ Gluten-free

Complete your plate: With a glass of Spicy Buttermilk (recipe on page 153).

4 cups sprouted mixed pulses (green gram, red *chana*, *moth*, dried green peas, white peas) or 1 cup uncooked mixed pulses (soak for 6–8 hours, drain and keep covered for another 12 hours)
1 cup tomato purée (or 3 medium tomatoes; grinded and sieved)
2 medium onions, chopped coarsely
8 garlic cloves, chopped finely
3 cloves
1 cinnamon stick
2-inch piece of ginger, chopped finely
5 dry red *Kashmiri* chillies
2 green chillies chopped
3 tsp *jeera* (cumin seeds)
4 whole black peppercorns
½ tsp turmeric powder
1 tbsp coriander powder
2 tbsp oil
Salt as per taste

VALUE PER SERVING		
Calories	239 kcal
Protein	12 gms
Fat	6 gms
Carbs	33 gms
Calcium	102 mgs
Fibre	4 gms
Iron	5 mgs

PAV BHAJI UNJUNKED

A healthy spin on the roadside favourite
– so good you'll never know the difference

Makes: 8 cups
Serving size: 1½ cups
Serves: 5–6

Pre-preparation time: 18–20 hrs
Preparation time: 10 mins
Cooking time: 30 mins

1½ cup *moong* sprouts or ½ cup
  uncooked green *moong* (soak
  for 6–8 hours, drain and keep
  covered for another 12 hours)
2 medium potatoes
1 cup green peas
¾ cup cauliflower,
  chopped coarsely
¾ cup French beans,
  chopped finely
¾ cup carrots, chopped finely
4 medium onions, chopped finely
4 medium tomatoes,
  chopped finely
2 medium capsicum,
  chopped finely
2 tbsp fresh coriander,
  chopped finely
12 large garlic cloves
3 dried red *Kashmiri* chillies
  (soak in hot water, let stand
  for 4 hours) or 2 tsp red
  chilli powder
1 tsp sugar
4 tsp *pav bhaji masala*
4 tsp salt (or as per taste)
Lemon juice as per taste
2 tbsp oil

1   Drain the water from the *Kashmiri* chillies.
2   Pressure-cook potatoes for 3 whistles; peel and grate.
3   Pressure-cook *moong* sprouts and peas for 2 whistles;
    mash coarsely.
4   Pressure-cook French beans, carrots and cauliflower
    for 1 whistle; mash coarsely.
5   In a blender, grind peeled garlic with 2 tbsp of chopped onions,
    Kashmiri chillies (or red chilli powder) and a pinch of salt with
    ⅓ cup water.
6   Heat the oil; sauté remaining onions for 2 minutes. Add
    capsicum; sauté for another 5 minutes.
7   Stir in the chilli-garlic paste; sauté till mixture leaves the
    sides of the pan.
8   Add tomatoes, *pav bhaji masala* and salt; sauté for
    3–4 minutes.
9   Add the potatoes along with remaining boiled and mashed
    vegetables, *moong* and peas along with 2 cups of water; cook
    for 5 minutes.
10 Add sugar and cook for another minute.
11 Add lemon juice just before serving. Garnish with fresh
    coriander.

• **Gluten-free**

Complete your plate: With multi-grain bread/*pav*/*chapatti* and a glass
of Spicy Buttermilk (recipe on page 153).

VALUE PER SERVING		
Calories	196 kcal
Protein	7.6 gms
Fat	5 gms
Carbs	29 gms
Calcium	88 mgs
Fibre	3 gms
Iron	2 mgs

BREAD CHAAT DETOXED

A nourishing twist on the popular Kolkata street food,
using whole-wheat bread and *moong* sprouts

Makes: 10 slices
Serving size: 2 slices
Serves: 5

Pre-preparation time: 18–20 hrs
Preparation time: 10 mins
Cooking time: 15 mins

1 Boil sprouts in water for 7–8 minutes. Drain and cool.
2 Combine all the ingredients in a bowl.
3 Cut one slice of bread into 6 equal pieces and arrange on a plate.
4 Place 1–2 drops of tamarind chutney on each piece, then spread ⅓ cup of the mixture over all.
5 Repeat for remaining slices.
6 Garnish with grated coconut, coriander and crushed peanuts; serve immediately.

⧖ **Quick & Easy**

Complete your plate: With a glass of Spicy Buttermilk (recipe on page 153).

10 slices whole-wheat or
   white bread (4"× 4")
1½ cups *moong* sprouts or ½ cup
   uncooked green *moong* (soak
   for 6–8 hours, drain and keep
   covered for another 12 hours)
2 large onions, chopped finely
2 large tomatoes, chopped finely
2 large potatoes, boiled and diced
1 cup cabbage, chopped finely
3–4 green chillies, chopped finely
3 tbsp Sweet Chutney
   (recipe in box)
¼ cup coconut, grated
¼ cup roasted peanuts,
   crushed coarsely
¼ cup fresh coriander,
   chopped finely
3 tsp *jeera* powder (cumin powder)
1 tsp red chilli powder
2 tsp salt (or as per taste)

Garnishing
¼ cup fresh coriander,
   chopped finely
¼ cup coconut, grated (optional)
¼ cup roasted peanuts, crushed
   coarsely (optional)

VALUE PER SERVING		
	Calories	401 kcal
	Protein	14 gms
	Fat	9.5 gms
	Carbs	65 gms
	Calcium	189 mgs
	Fibre	2 gms
	Iron	2 mgs

SWEET CHUTNEY

Makes: ¼ cup

1 cup (100 gms) dates
2 tsp *jeera* powder
   (cumin powder)
2 tsp red chilli powder
½ tsp black salt
2 tbsp sugar
Salt as per taste

1 Soak dates in 1 cup of boiling water for 10–15 minutes; allow to cool.
2 Mash by hand, then sieve and add ½ cup water.
3 Transfer to a pan, add remaining ingredients and boil for about 5 minutes.
4 Cool before serving.

RICE and VEGETABLE BAKE

A bed of beans, carrots, peppers and salsa
topped with a layer of rice in white sauce

Makes: 6 cups
Serving size: 2 cups
Serves: 3

Preparation time: 10 mins
Cooking time: 30 mins

1 Cook the rice in boiling water. Drain and keep aside to cool.
2 Bring 3 cups of water to boil and drop in the tomatoes to blanch. When the skins start to peel, remove and cool. Discard the skins and chop tomatoes finely.
3 Pressure-cook the French beans and carrots for 1 whistle, drain and keep aside.
4 Preheat the oven at 160°C for 7–10 minutes.
5 Heat 1 tbsp oil in a pan and sauté the bell peppers for 1 minute.
6 Add the boiled carrots and French beans; sauté for 2 minutes. Keep aside.
7 Grind the onion, garlic, turmeric, red chilli powder and coriander powder together.
8 In a separate pan, heat 1 tbsp oil and sauté the onion paste, for about 5 minutes, until it leaves the sides of the pan.
9 Add the blanched tomatoes and sauté for 5 more minutes.
10 Add the sautéed vegetables, baked beans and salt.
11 Add ketchup, salsa, oregano, basil, chilli flakes and cook for 1 minute; set aside.
12 Combine the white sauce with the cooked rice.
13 In a baking dish, first spread the vegetables. Top with a layer of rice.
14 Bake in preheated oven for 10 minutes.

❧ **Gluten-free**

A complete plate!

2 cups Low-Fat White Sauce
   (recipe on page 109)
¾ uncooked cup rice
1 cup canned baked beans,
   with minimum sauce
2 large tomatoes
1 medium onion, chopped finely
¼ cup carrots, chopped finely
¼ cup French beans,
   chopped finely
1 small yellow bell pepper,
   chopped finely
1 small red bell pepper,
   chopped finely
4 garlic cloves, peeled and halved
1 tsp red chilli powder
1 tsp coriander powder
½ tsp turmeric powder
1 tsp *jeera* (cumin seeds)
2 tbsp readymade salsa
1 tbsp ketchup
1 tsp red chilli flakes
½ tsp dried basil
½ tsp dried oregano

VALUE PER SERVING		
	Calories	372 kcal
	Protein	13.5 gms
	Fat	9.7 gms
	Carbs	38 gms
	Calcium	332 mgs
	Fibre	3 gms
	Iron	4 mgs

PASTA and BEANS in RED SAUCE

Baked beans, corn, bell peppers and pasta in a tangy
tomato sauce with a yummy cheese crust on top

Makes: 8 cups
Serving size: 2 cups
Serves: 4

Preparation time: 5 mins
Cooking time: 30 mins

1½ cups uncooked pasta
(macaroni, farfalle or fusilli)
1 can (400 gms) baked beans
½ cup fresh corn (from cob) or
sweet corn kernels
½ large red bell pepper, sliced
½ large capsicum, sliced
½ large yellow bell pepper, sliced
3 large tomatoes
1 large onion, sliced
1½ tsp red chilli powder
50 gms low-fat cheese, grated
⅓ cup ketchup
3 garlic cloves, chopped finely
2 tbsp mixed dried herbs (optional)
1 tsp salt or as per taste
3 tsp oil

1   Heat 1 tsp oil and sauté the onions and bell peppers for
    3 minutes. Divide this mix into two equal portions; set aside.
2   Pressure-cook the corn for 5 whistles and set aside.
3   Place the pasta and tomatoes in boiling water in the same pot.
4   After 5 minutes, remove the tomatoes; cool.
5   Continue boiling the pasta until it is done; drain and rinse with
    cold water. Set aside.
6   Once tomatoes are cooled, peel the skins and finely chop
    the flesh.
7   Preheat oven at 160°C for 7–10 minutes.
8   Heat 2 tsp oil and sauté garlic for half a minute. Add 1 portion
    of the onion-bell pepper mixture. Stir in red chilli powder and
    sauté for 10 seconds.
9   Add the tomatoes and 1 tsp salt; cook for 3 minutes.
10 Add the boiled corn and baked beans; cook for 1 minute.
11 Mix in the pasta, tomato ketchup and half of the grated
    cheese; simmer for 2 minutes. For desired consistency add
    ½ cup of water. Adjust salt as per taste.
12 Spread the pasta mix in a greased baking dish and top with
    the remaining portion of the onion-bell pepper mix. Sprinkle
    with mixed dried herbs.
13 Garnish with the remaining grated cheese.
14 Bake in preheated oven for about 10 minutes. Serve hot.

VALUE PER SERVING		
Calories	286 kcal
Protein	13 gms
Fat	5 gms
Carbs	60 gms
Calcium	173 mgs
Fibre	2 gms
Iron	3 mgs

A complete plate!

RED CHANA BIRYANI

The all-time favourite comfort food with traditional
veggies plus a special addition – red *chana*

Makes: 12 cups	Pre-preparation time: 6–8 hrs
Serving size: 2 cups	Preparation time: 10 mins
Serves: 6	Cooking time: 50 mins

1 Rinse the rice and soak for 20 minutes.
2 Pressure-cook the *chana* for 8–10 whistles.
3 Heat *ghee* in a pan; add the *jeera*. Once the seeds begin to splutter, add red chillies, bay leaves, cloves, cardamom pods and cinnamon sticks. Sauté for 1 minute over a low flame.
4 Add rice, 4 cups of water and 1 tsp salt. Cover and cook over a low flame.
5 When the rice is half cooked, add saffron along with the water in which it was soaked; add lemon juice. Cover and cook until all the water dries up. (Keep checking that rice does not get burnt at the bottom.)
6 Remove from heat and cool. Discard the red chillies, bay leaves, cloves, cardamom pods and cinnamon sticks.
7 For the garlic paste, grind the ingredients together in a blender.
8 Heat 2 tsp oil and sauté the paste for 5 minutes.
9 Stir in the tomato purée and add 1 tsp salt; sauté for another 8 minutes.
10 Add the boiled *chana*, carrots, beans, peas and curd; cook for 5–7 minutes.
11 Add sugar and remove from heat.
12 In a separate pan, heat 1 tsp oil and sauté the onion until dark brown.

continued on next page…

1½ cups rice, uncooked
½ cup uncooked red *chana*
    (soak for 6–8 hours)
¼ cup French beans, chopped finely
¼ cup carrots, chopped finely
¼ cup green peas
1 large onion, sliced
1 cup tomato purée (made
    from 3 large tomatoes)
⅓ cup fresh curd, made from
    toned milk (3.5% fat)
1 tsp sugar
2 cardamom pods
2 cinnamon sticks
2 cloves
½ tsp *jeera* (cumin seeds)
3 bay leaves
2 dry red chillies
1½ tsp lemon juice (juice
    of ½ lemon)
Pinch of saffron, soaked
    in 2 tbsp water
1 tbsp *ghee*
3 tsp oil
2 tsp salt or as per taste

Garlic paste
7 large garlic cloves, chopped finely
2 green chillies, chopped finely
1 tsp red chilli powder
1-inch piece of ginger, chopped finely
2 tbsp coriander powder
2 tbsp water

RED CHANA BIRYANI

To serve

1 Preheat the oven at 160°C for 7–10 minutes.
2 In a baking dish, first spread the *chana*.
3 Top with the rice.
4 Garnish with the sautéed onions and bake in pre-heated oven for 5–7 minutes. Serve hot.

● **Gluten-free**

Complete your plate: With a bowl of Mint *Raita* (recipe on page 137).

VALUE PER SERVING		
Calories	263 kcal
Protein	8 gms
Fat	5 gms
Carbs	23 gms
Calcium	72 mgs
Fibre	2 gms
Iron	2 mgs

MINT RAITA

A simple mint-and-curd concoction
that will add zest to any meal

Makes: 3 cups
Serving size: ¾ cup
Serves: 4

Pre-preparation time: 30 mins
Preparation time: 30 mins
Cooking time: 5 mins

4 cups low-fat curd; made
   from 800 ml double toned milk
   (1.5% fat)
4 tbsp fresh mint leaves,
   chopped finely
2 small green chillies,
   chopped finely
½ tsp black pepper powder
1 large onion, chopped finely
½ tsp *jeera* powder
   (cumin powder)
1½ tsp sugar
¼ tsp red chilli powder
Salt as per taste

1 Hang the curd in a muslin cloth for half an hour.
2 Remove the excess water and transfer thickened curd
   to a bowl.
3 Add the remaining ingredients and mix well.
4 Garnish with red chilli powder and serve chilled.

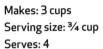

- Gluten-free
- Quick & Easy

VALUE PER SERVING		
Calories	60 kcal
Protein	4 gms
Fat	0 gm
Carbs	10 gms
Calcium	198 mgs
Fibre	0 gm
Iron	1 mg

EGG and MUSHROOM CURRY

A hot and spicy red curry that swaps
boiled egg whites for whole eggs

Makes: 8 cups
Serving size: 1½ cups
Serves: 6

Preparation time: 5 mins
Cooking time: 35 mins

12 eggs
16 large mushrooms, sliced thickly
6 large tomatoes, sliced thickly
4 medium onions, sliced thickly
5 garlic cloves, chopped finely
6 green chillies, halved
2 tsp red chilli powder
2 tsp *jeera* powder (cumin powder)
½ tsp black pepper powder
   (optional)
½ tsp *garam masala*
1 tsp salt and as per taste
4 tbsp oil

1   Hard-boil the eggs. Remove the shells and slice each egg
    into half; scoop out and discard the yolks.
2   Heat 1 tbsp oil in a pan; add onions and sauté for 2 minutes.
    Stir in green chillies and garlic; sauté for another minute.
3   Add tomatoes; sauté for 5 minutes. Remove from heat and
    cool completely.
4   Heat 1 tbsp oil and sauté mushrooms for 5 minutes. Set aside.
5   Mix in the red chilli powder into the onion and tomato mix.
    In a blender, grind to a smooth paste.
6   Heat 2 tbsp oil in a pan and cook the paste for 4 minutes.
    Add 1 tsp salt and cook for another 5 minutes, stirring
    occasionally.
7   Meanwhile, bring 3 cups of water to the boil.
8   To the paste, add *garam masala, jeera* powder and black
    pepper powder; cook until the gravy leaves the sides of the
    pan, approximately 5 minutes.
9   Mix in the boiling water; cook for 2 minutes.
10 Finally, add the boiled egg whites, sautéed mushrooms and
    salt as per taste, and cook for 2 minutes.
11 Garnish with fresh coriander. Serve hot. Each serving should
    comprise 2 full egg whites (4 pieces).

VALUE PER SERVING		
Calories	181 kcal
Protein	10 gms
Fat	10 gms
Carbs	10 gms
Calcium	93 mgs
Fibre	1 gm
Iron	2 mgs

● **Gluten-free**

Complete your plate: With a cup of steamed rice.

CORN RAJMA BHEL

The lip-smacking flavours of *bhel* get
a boost with corn and kidney beans

Makes: 8 cups	Pre-preparation time: 6–8 hrs
Serving size: 2 cups	Preparation time: 20 mins
Serves: 4	Cooking time: 20 mins

1 Pressure-cook the *rajma* with 4 cups of water and ½ tsp salt
  and for 4 whistles. Strain and keep aside.

2 Pressure-cook the corn for 6 whistles. Strain and keep aside.

3 Melt butter in a pan. Sauté onion, capsicum and green chillies
  for 4 minutes.

4 Add corn, *rajma*, potatoes, *chaat masala*, black pepper
  powder and 1 tsp salt; sauté for 3 minutes.

5 Remove from heat; add lemon juice, Feta cheese, sugar and
  coriander.

⌛ **Quick & Easy**

Complete your plate: With a glass of Spicy Buttermilk (recipe on page 153).

1 cup uncooked *rajma* (kidney
  beans; soak for 6–8 hours)
2 cups fresh corn (from cob) or
  sweet corn kernels
2 medium potatoes, boiled,
  peeled and diced
2 medium capsicum,
  chopped finely
2 medium onions, chopped finely
4 green chillies, chopped finely
4 tbsp fresh coriander,
  chopped finely
1 tsp *chaat masala*
¼ tsp black pepper powder
75 gms Feta cheese
Juice of 1 lemon
2 tbsp sugar
2 tbsp butter
Salt as per taste

VALUE PER SERVING		
	Calories	362 kcal
	Protein	15 gms
	Fat	9 gms
	Carbs	56 gms
	Calcium	154 mgs
	Fibre	3 gms
	Iron	4 mgs

SNACKS

SEV PURI DETOXED

A *chaat*-inspired salad you can pop
in your mouth without worry

Makes: 25 pieces
Serving size: 5 pieces
Serves: 5

Pre-preparation time: 18–20 hrs
Preparation time: 15 mins
Cooking time: 35 mins

2 cups fresh curd; made from
   toned milk (3.5% fat)
25 slices of cucumber,
   approximately 0.5 cm
   in thickness (should be cut
   just before serving)
1 cup *moong* sprouts or ⅓ cup
   uncooked green *moong* (soak
   for 6–8 hours, drain and keep
   covered for another 12 hours)
1 small onion, chopped finely
1 green chilli, chopped finely
½ tsp *chaat masala*
1 tsp powdered sugar
½ tsp *jeera* powder
   (cumin powder)
¼ tsp black pepper powder
½ tsp red chilli powder
Salt as per taste

1 Hang the curd in a muslin cloth for half hour to drain
   excess water.

2 Meanwhile, boil 300 ml of water with ½ tsp of salt.
   Add *moong* sprouts, remove from heat and cover. Drain after
   20 minutes and let it cool.

3 Remove the thick curd from the cloth and transfer to a bowl.

4 Add sprouts, onion or tomato, fresh coriander, green chilli,
   sugar, pepper and salt.

5 Spread the cucumber slices on a serving dish. Ladle spoonfuls
   of the mixture on the slices.

6 Garnish with Green Chutney (optional, recipe on page 152),
   chaat masala, jeera powder, red chilli powder and fresh
   coriander. Serve immediately.

✻ **Jain**: Don't sprout the *moong*, and replace onion with a small tomato.
● **Gluten-free**
⏳ **Quick & Easy**

VALUE PER SERVING		
	Calories	115 kcal
	Protein	6.5 gms
	Fat	3.5 gms
	Carbs	14 gms
	Calcium	156 mgs
	Fibre	1 gm
	Iron	1.2 mgs

STEAMED DAHI VADAS

With the same great taste as the original, these guilt-free *vadas* will keep you coming back for more

Makes: 12 *vadas*
Serving size: 2 *vadas*
Serves: 6

Pre-preparation time: 2 hrs
Preparation time: 5 mins
Cooking time: 40 mins

1. Hang the curd in a muslin cloth for at least half an hour.
2. Rinse and drain soaked dal. Grind in blender with spinach, ginger, green chilli, coriander seeds, *saunf, hing*, salt, oil and 1 tbsp water.
3. Beat the batter, ensuring you move the spoon only in one direction, for 2–3 minutes.
4. Grease plates of *idli* maker with some oil. Pour water into the *idli* maker; once it comes to the boil, add fruit salt to the batter, stirring continuously for half a minute.
5. Immediately pour batter into the greased plates. Steam for 15 minutes. Remove the plates and allow to cool.
6. Meanwhile, remove curd from cloth; add sugar, *jeera* powder, *chaat masala* and salt.
7. Once cooled, remove *vadas* from the *idli* plates using a sharp knife. Arrange on a platter. Spread the curd over the *vadas* and top with fresh coriander. If desired, garnish with grated carrots.

✻ **Jain**: Omit ginger.
● **Gluten-free**

½ cup uncooked split green *moong* dal (soak for 2 hours)
8–10 fresh spinach leaves
1½ litres low-fat curd, made from double-toned milk (1.5% fat)
1 tsp fruit salt (Eno)
3 tsp sugar, powdered
3–4 green chillies
1-inch piece of ginger
2 tsp coriander seeds
2 tbsp fresh coriander, chopped finely
1 tsp *saunf* (aniseed)
2 pinches *hing* (asafoetida)
½ tsp *chaat masala*
½ tsp *jeera* powder (cumin powder)
1 tsp of oil
1 tsp salt

VALUE PER SERVING		
	Calories	178 kcal
	Protein	13 gms
	Fat	2.2 gms
	Carbs	26 gms
	Calcium	413 mgs
	Fibre	0.6 gm
	Iron	1 mg

HANDVA

Loaded with fresh vegetables, this savoury
steamed cake is a Gujarati speciality

Makes: 8 slices
Serving size: 1 slice
Serves: 8

Preparation time: 5 mins
Cooking time: 25 mins

1 cup *rawa* (semolina)
½ cup *besan* (gram flour)
¼ cup carrots, chopped finely
1 small capsicum, chopped finely
1 small onion, chopped finely
¼ cup bottle gourd, chopped finely
½ cup peas
½ cup sweet corn kernels
1 green chilli, chopped finely
1½ tbsp sugar
1 tbsp coriander leaves,
    chopped finely
1 tsp fruit salt (Eno)
Juice of 2 lemons
Salt as per taste
1 tsp mustard seeds
¼ tsp turmeric powder
8–10 curry leaves
2 dry red chillies, broken
1 tsp red chilli powder
1 tbsp oil

1   In a large bowl, combine *rawa, besan*, chopped vegetables,
    corn, peas, salt, sugar, green chilli, coriander leaves and lemon
    juice. This forms the *handva* batter.

2   Pour water in a *dhokla* maker/pressure cooker (without lid)
    and bring to the boil.

3   Grease a heavy-bottomed pan (6-inch in diameter and
    about 2-inch deep) with some oil and keep aside.

4   In a separate pan, heat oil. Add mustard seeds. Once seeds
    begin to splutter, turn off the flame.

5   Immediately add dry red chillies, curry leaves, turmeric
    powder, red chilli powder and 1 cup water. Add this to the
    handva batter.

6   Once the water in the *dhokla* maker/pressure cooker
    is boiling, add fruit salt to the *handva* batter and mix the
    batter for 10 seconds till fluffy.

7   Immediately pour the batter into the greased pan and spread
    into an even layer.

8   Steam for 20 minutes. (If using a pressure cooker, remove
    the whistle before closing the lid.)

9   Cut into 8 slices and serve with Green Chutney (recipe on
    page 152).

VALUE PER SERVING		
	Calories	125 kcal
	Protein	4 gms
	Fat	2 gms
	Carbs	22 gms
	Calcium	16 mgs
	Fibre	1 gm
	Iron	2 mgs

⧖ **Quick & Easy**

GREEN DHOKLA

Spongy, savoury cakes made with green gram and spinach…
the perfect snack to keep you going until dinner

Makes: 28–30 pieces
Serving size: 4 pieces
(1½" × 1½" each)
Serves 7

Pre-preparation time: 6–8 hrs
Preparation time: 5 mins
Cooking time: 35 mins

1 cup uncooked green *moong*
(soak for 6–8 hours)
2 bundles of spinach
(approximately 200 gms
after cleaning)
2-inch piece of ginger
5–6 green chillies
1 tbsp sugar
1 tbsp lemon juice
1 tsp fruit salt (Eno)
3 tsp salt (or as per taste)
2 tsp oil

1 Drain and rinse *moong*.
2 In a blender, grind *moong*, green chillies, ginger, spinach, lime
   juice, oil, salt and sugar with ¼ cup water to a smooth paste.
   Check consistency to achieve a semi-thick paste, adding more
   water if required. Set aside.
3 Lightly grease the plates (8-inch diameter) of *dhokla* maker.
4 Pour water in the *dhokla* maker/pressure cooker; once it
   comes to the boil, add ½ tsp fruit salt to half the batter and
   stir. Immediately pour into prepared plate.
5 Steam for 15 minutes. (If using a pressure cooker, remove the
   whistle before closing the lid.)
6 Repeat for remaining batter. Add fruit salt just before pouring
   the batter into plates, as this will prevent loss of volume.
7 When cooled, cut into square pieces (1½" × 1½") but do not
   remove from the plate.

For tempering
1 tsp mustard seeds
½ tsp white sesame seeds
2 tbsp fresh coconut, grated
2 tsp oil
1½ tbsp lemon juice
1 tbsp sugar
½ tsp salt

For tempering
1 In half cup water, mix sugar, lemon juice and salt.
2 Heat oil in a pan; add mustard and sesame seeds. Once seeds
   begin to splutter, turn off flame and add the water mixture.
3 Spread this evenly over the *dhoklas* in the plate. Let it soak
   for 10 minutes.

continued on next page…

VALUE PER SERVING		
Calories	133 kcal
Protein	7 gms
Fat	3 gms
Carbs	20 gms
Calcium	50 mgs
Fibre	1 gm
Iron	1.5 mgs

GREEN DHOKLA

To serve

1   Garnish with grated coconut.
2   Serve with Green Chutney (recipe in box on page 152).

✳ **Jain**: Omit ginger.
◗ **Gluten-free**

GREEN CHUTNEY

Makes: 1¼ cups

5–6 green chillies
2 cups fresh coriander
1-inch piece of ginger
1 tbsp roasted peanuts
Juice of 1½ lemons
2 tbsp water
Salt as per taste

1   Grind all the ingredients together in a blender to make a smooth paste.

SPICY BUTTERMILK

A sweet and spicy drink made with low-fat curd

Makes: 6 glasses	Preparation time: 5 mins
Serving size: 1 glass	Cooking time: 5 mins
Serves 6	

1 Place the curd, water, sugar, salt, green chilli, ginger and *jeera* powder in a vessel. Churn with a hand blender and strain.

2 Heat oil in a small pan. Add *jeera* and mustard seeds; once they begin to splutter, add to the prepared buttermilk.

3 Serve in a tall glass. Garnish with coriander.

✳ **Jain**: Omit ginger.

◗ **Gluten-free**

⧖ **Quick & Easy**

2 cups fat-free curd, made from
400 ml fat-free milk (0–0.8% fat)
4 cups water
2 tsp powdered sugar
1½ tsp salt
1 green chilli, chopped finely
½-inch piece of ginger,
    chopped finely
½ tsp *jeera* powder
    (cumin powder)
½ tsp *jeera* (cumin seeds)
½ tsp mustard seeds
1 tbsp fresh coriander leaves,
    finely chopped
1 tsp oil

VALUE PER SERVING		
Calories	36 kcal
Protein	2 gms
Fat	1 gm
Carbs	5 gms
Calcium	89 mgs
Fibre	0 gm
Iron	0 mg

VADA PAV UNJUNKED

The same great taste of a *vada pav*, but fortified
with *paneer* and baked, not fried

Makes: 8 toasts
Serving size: 1 toast
Serves 8

Preparation time: 10 mins
Cooking time: 10 mins

8 slices whole-wheat or
white bread (4"× 4") or
french baguette
1 litre double toned milk
(1.5% fat)
4 medium potatoes, boiled,
peeled and diced
2 garlic cloves, chopped finely
2 green chillies, chopped finely
10–15 curry leaves, chopped
2 tbsp coriander leaves,
chopped finely
½ tsp mustard seeds
¼ tsp turmeric powder
Juice of 2 lemons
Salt as per taste
1 tbsp oil

1   Bring milk to the boil and turn off flame. Immediately add
    juice of 1 lemon and stir until milk curdles. Strain through
    a muslin cloth, making sure all the liquid or whey is removed.
    What remains in the cloth is *paneer*.

2   Preheat the oven at 160°C for 7–10 minutes.

3   Heat the oil in a pan. Add mustard seeds; once the seeds begin
    to splutter, tip in the garlic, green chillies and curry leaves.
    Sauté for half a minute.

4   Add potatoes, turmeric powder and salt. Mix well.

5   Transfer to a large plate and cool.

6   Crumble the *paneer* and combine with the potato mix, along
    with coriander and juice of 1 lemon.

7   Mash this mixture lightly by hand and divide into 8 portions.

8   Lightly toast the bread. Spread the mixture on the toasted
    bread and bake in preheated oven for 4–5 minutes. Serve hot.

⧗ Quick & Easy

Complete your plate: With a glass of Spicy Buttermilk (recipe on page 153).

VALUE PER SERVING		
Calories	158 kcal
Protein	7 gms
Fat	2 gms
Carbs	28 gms
Calcium	165 mgs
Fibre	2 gms
Iron	1 mg

HARA BHARA KEBAB

An old-time favourite… Roasted *chana* dal-cakes loaded
with spinach for a healthy and satisfying snack

Makes 42 kebabs
Serving size: 6 kebabs
Serves 7

Pre-preparation time: 2–3 hrs
Preparation time: 5 mins
Cooking time: 25 mins

½ cup uncooked *chana* dal
  (soak for 2–3 hours)
4 bundles spinach (approximately
500 gms after cleaning)
2 medium potatoes, boiled
  and mashed
3 garlic cloves, chopped finely
8 green chillies, halved
2-inch piece of ginger,
  chopped finely
2 tsp *amchur* powder
  (dry mango powder)
½ tsp *jeera* powder
  (cumin powder)
1 tsp *chaat masala*
3 tsp lemon juice
2 tbsp oil
Salt as per taste

1 Drain and rinse the *chana* dal. Pressure-cook with 2 cups
  of water for 2 whistles. Drain and set aside.

2 Clean and wash the spinach well, remove the stems and
  place in a large pan. Sprinkle with some water, cover and cook
  for 10 minutes.

3 Grind the cooked *chana* dal with ginger and green chillies
  to a smooth paste.

4 Drain the spinach to remove any excess water. Once cooled,
  grind separately in a blender.

5 Mix together the *chana* dal paste, spinach paste, mash
  potatoes, *jeera* powder, *chaat masala*, *amchur* powder.

6 Heat ½ tsp oil and sauté garlic for 30 seconds. Add to the
  above mixture.

7 Divide into 42 equal portions. Shape each portion into
  a round ball and flatten it to make kebabs.

8 Roast the kebabs on a non-stick *tawa* using the remaining oil,
  until evenly browned on both sides.

9 Serve with Green Chutney (recipe on page 152) and Low-Fat
  Mayo (recipe on page 109).

VALUE PER SERVING		
	Calories	136 kcal
	Protein	5 gms
	Fat	4 gms
	Carbs	19 gms
	Calcium	72 mgs
	Fibre	2 gms
	Iron	1 mg

• **Gluten-free**

CHICKPEA CHAAT

The kick of chilli, the tang of *chaat masala* – this
hot-and-sour salad is a treat for the taste buds

Makes 6 cups	Pre-preparation time: 6–8 hrs
Serving size: 1 cup	Preparation time: 5 mins
Serves 6	Cooking time: 15 mins

1 Pressure-cook chickpeas with 3 cups of water
  for 6–7 whistles.
2 Blanch the capsicum in boiling water for about 2 minutes.
  Drain and cool.
3 Combine the boiled chickpeas, chopped vegetables,
  blanched capsicum, green chillies, fresh coriander,
  chaat masala, lemon juice and salt.
4 Mix well and serve.

✻ **Jain:** Replace the onion and potato with 1 cup chopped cabbage.
• **Gluten-free**
⧗ **Quick & Easy**

1 cup uncooked chickpeas
  (soak for 6–8 hours)
1 large tomato, chopped finely
1 large onion, chopped finely
1 medium capsicum,
  chopped finely
1 medium potato, boiled,
  peeled and diced
3–4 tbsp fresh coriander,
  chopped finely
2 green chillies, chopped finely
3 tsp lemon juice
2 tbsp *chaat masala*
Salt as per taste

VALUE PER SERVING		
	Calories	113 kcal
	Protein	5 gms
	Fat	1.5 gms
	Carbs	20 gms
	Calcium	70 mgs
	Fibre	1.4 gms
	Iron	1.5 mgs

QUESADILLA

A no-junk take on the traditional Mexican dish,
with a filling of corn, beans and mushroom

Makes: 7 quesadillas
Serving size: 1 quesadilla
Serves 7

Preparation time: 10 mins
Cooking time: 30 mins

1½ cups *maida* (all-purpose flour)
1¼ cups whole-wheat flour
1 tsp oil (to add to dough)
1 tbsp butter (for roasting
 the wraps)
1 cup fresh corn (from cob) or
 sweet corn kernels
1 can (400 gms) baked beans
9 large mushrooms, chopped finely
¼ cup cold double-toned milk
 (1.5% fat)
1 tbsp cornflour
½ tsp black pepper powder
½ tsp red chilli flakes
½ tsp sugar
2 tsp butter
Salt as per taste
10 tbsp grated cheese (optional)

1 Put the mushrooms in boiling water for 2 minutes. Strain and
   squeeze out excess water. Chop finely. Keep aside.

2 Pressure-cook the corn with 3 cups of water and ½ tsp salt
   for 5 whistles and strain. Keep aside.

3 Once cooled, give the corn a quick whisk in the mixer, so that
   the kernels are crushed but not puréed.

4 Strain and discard the purée from the can of baked beans
   and mash the beans.

5 Heat butter and sauté the corn for 4 minutes.

6 Add mushrooms and sauté for 2–3 minutes.

7 Season with pepper and salt as per taste.

8 Dissolve the cornflour in cold milk and add to the above
   mixture. Cook for 3 minutes.

9 Add the mashed beans, sugar and chilli flakes. Cook for
   4 minutes till most of the liquid evaporates. Remove from heat.

10 Divide this mixture into 7 equal parts and keep aside.

11 Knead a dough by combining the wheat flour, *maida*, 1 tsp oil,
   and water as required.

12 Divide the dough into 14 equal parts and roll out thin wraps
   with each part.

13 Partially roast all the wraps on a *tawa* without using any oil.

14 Spread one part of the mixture evenly on one wrap. Top with
   2 tbsp of grated cheese (optional). Place another wrap over
   this and press down firmly.
   continued on next page…

VALUE PER SERVING		
Calories	268 kcal
Protein	10 gms
Fat	4 gms
Carbs	46 gms
Calcium	97 mgs
Fibre	2 gms
Iron	3 mgs

QUESADILLA

15 Using a small amount of butter, roast on a heated *tawa* until brown spots appear on the surface. Flip over and repeat for the other side.

16 Cut into 8 slices and serve immediately with Red Garlic Sauce (recipe in box).

✳ Jain
❧ Gluten-free

RED GARLIC SAUCE

Makes: ¼ cup
Preparation time: 5 mins
Cooking time: 10 mins

25 large garlic cloves
   (approximately 25 gms),
   chopped coarsely
8 large green chillies
   (approximately 25 gms),
   chopped coarsely
½ cup tomato ketchup
1 tbsp oil
Salt as per taste

1 Grind garlic and green chillies together in a mixer to a coarse consistency.
2 Heat the oil; sauté the mixture for a minute.
3 Add salt; sauté for another 5 minutes.
4 Add ketchup and simmer for 2 minutes. Cool to room temperature and serve.

THANDAI

A sweetened milk-based drink
fortified with dry fruit

Makes 4 glasses	Pre-preparation time: 8–10 hrs
Serving size: 1 glass	Preparation time: 5 mins
Serves 4	Cooking time: 5 mins

1 Soak dates, figs, almonds, cardamom and *saunf* in 1½ cups of water overnight (8–10 hours).
2 Skin the almonds and remove cardamom seeds from cardamom pods.
3 Grind them with the remaining soaked ingredients to a paste, along with the water in which they were soaked.
4 To make the *thandai*, add 1½ tbsp of the paste to 200 ml cold milk and add 1½ tsp sugar. Stir well and serve chilled.

✳ Jain
● Gluten-free
⌛ Quick & Easy

4 seedless dates
4 dry figs
4 green cardamom pods
10 almonds
1 tsp *saunf* (aniseed)
6 tsp powdered sugar
800 ml fat-free milk (0–0.8% fat)

VALUE PER SERVING		
	Calories	129 kcal
	Protein	8 gms
	Fat	1 gm
	Carbs	22 gms
	Calcium	324 mgs
	Fibre	1 gm
	Iron	1 mg

VEGGIE ALFREDO TOAST

Exotic vegetables drenched in a low-fat white sauce, spread over whole-wheat bread and baked to crisp perfection

Makes 7 toasts
Serving size: 1 toast
Serves 7

Preparation time: 10 mins
Cooking time: 25 mins

1 Heat oil. Sauté garlic for a few seconds.
2 Add onions and sauté until translucent.
3 Add carrot, baby corn and ½ tsp salt; sauté for 2 minutes.
4 Add bell peppers; sauté for 1 minute.
5 Then add cabbage and mushroom; sauté for 2 minutes.
6 Add broccoli and cook for another minute.
7 Preheat oven at 160°C for 7–10 minutes.
8 Stir in ¼ cup milk and cook for a minute.
9 Dissolve corn flour in the remaining ¼ cup of milk and add to above preparation along with salt and pepper.
10 Add mayonnaise and grated cheese, cooking until the mixture thickens.
11 Finally, add oregano and chilli flakes. Remove from heat.
12 Divide the mixture into 7 equal portions and spread over bread slices. Bake for 10 minutes. Serve hot with a glass of *Thandai* (recipe on page 163).

⌛ **Quick & Easy**

7 slices whole-wheat or
   white bread (4"× 4")
1 cup mushrooms, chopped finely
¼ cup carrot, chopped finely
¼ cup red bell pepper,
   chopped finely
¼ cup baby corn, chopped finely
¼ cup cabbage, chopped finely
¼ cup tiny broccoli florets
1 medium onion, chopped finely
2 garlic cloves, chopped finely
100 ml fat-free milk (0–0.8% fat)
2 tbsp readymade low-fat
   mayonnaise
35 gms low-fat cheese, grated
1 tbsp corn flour
1 tsp red chilli flakes
½ tsp dried oregano
¼ tsp black pepper powder
Salt as per taste
1 tbsp olive oil

VALUE PER SERVING		
Calories	109 kcal
Protein	5 gms
Fat	2.6 gms
Carbs	16 gms
Calcium	79 mgs
Fibre	1 gm
Iron	2 mgs

LEBANESE PIZZA

A Tahina-free 'red hummus' replaces tomato sauce
in this cheesy, bell-pepper-and-onion-topped pizza

Makes 4 pizzas (24 slices)
Serving size: 3 slices
Serves 8

Pre-preparation time: 6–8 hrs
Preparation time: 5 mins
Cooking time: 40 mins

1 Soak the *Kashmiri* chillies in warm water for 10 minutes.
2 Blanch the tomato. When cooled, chop into big pieces.
3 Pressure-cook the chickpeas with some salt and 3 cups
   of water for 7–8 whistles. Drain and cool.
4 Meanwhile, preheat the oven at 160°C for 7–10 minutes.
5 For the chilli hummus, grind chickpeas, chillies, basil, chopped
   tomato and garlic to a smooth paste in a blender. Add salt
   and hot and sweet tomato ketchup. Divide into 4 parts.
6 Spread 1 part of the hummus on pizza bread and top with
   onion, bell peppers and cheese.
7 Bake in preheated oven for 10 minutes. Cut each pizza
   into 6 slices. Serve hot.

4 whole-wheat, thin-crust pizza
  bases or pita breads
½ cup uncooked chickpeas
  (soak for 6–8 hrs)
5 large fresh basil leaves,
  chopped finely
4 large cloves of garlic,
  chopped finely
3 dry red *Kashmiri* chillies
3 tbsp readymade hot and
  sweet sauce
1 yellow bell pepper,
  chopped finely
1 medium onion, chopped finely
1 medium tomato
50 gms low-fat cheese, grated
Salt as per taste

VALUE PER SERVING		
	Calories	182 kcal
	Protein	7 gms
	Fat	2 gms
	Carbs	34 gms
	Calcium	93 mgs
	Fibre	1 gm
	Iron	2 mgs

PESTO PANEER BRUSCHETTA

Crunchy baguette slices layered with pesto and a tomato,
basil and cottage cheese topping

Makes 18 bruschettas	**Preparation time: 5 mins**
Serving size: 2 bruschettas	**Cooking time: 25 mins**
Serves 9	

1 For the pesto, combine all the ingredients and blend at high speed to make a smooth paste. Set aside.
2 Preheat the oven at 160°C for 7–10 minutes.
3 Bring milk to the boil and turn off flame. Immediately add lemon juice and stir until milk curdles. Strain through a muslin cloth, making sure all the liquid or whey is removed. What remains in the cloth is *paneer*.
4 To make a *paneer* diskette, press down on the *paneer* by placing a flat weight over it while it is in the muslin cloth. Let stand 30 minutes, then remove the diskette from the muslin cloth and cut into small cubes.
5 In a bowl, combine *paneer*, tomatoes, basil leaves, olive oil, cheese, salt and black pepper powder. Toss gently.
6 Toast the baguette slices in preheated oven for 7 minutes.
7 Apply a thin layer of pesto on each slice. Divide the *paneer* mixture equally and spoon over the slices. Serve immediately.

⧖ **Quick & Easy**

1 French baguette, cut into
    18 slices
1 litre fat-free milk (0–0.8% fat)
8–10 fresh basil leaves,
    chopped finely
2 medium tomatoes,
    chopped finely
2 tbsp low-fat cheese, grated
2 tsp olive oil
3 tsp lemon juice (juice of 1 lemon)
Black pepper powder as per taste
Salt as per taste

Pesto
1 cup fresh basil leaves,
    chopped finely
¼ cup olive oil
5 garlic cloves, chopped finely
1½ tbsp walnuts, chopped finely
35 gms low-fat cheese, grated
½ tsp black pepper powder
Salt as per taste

VALUE PER SERVING		
Calories	179 kcal
Protein	7 gms
Fat	6 gms
Carbs	24 gms
Calcium	193 mgs
Fibre	0.5 gm
Iron	1 mg

BREAD ROLLS

Bread slices slathered with a hummus-like chickpea dip,
topped with veggies, rolled up and grilled golden-brown

Makes 12 rolls
Serving size: 2 rolls
Serves 6

Pre-preparation time: 6–8 hrs
Preparation time: 5 mins
Cooking time: 20 mins

12 slices white bread
1½ cups carrots, grated finely
1½ cups cabbage, sliced finely
½ cup uncooked chickpeas
   (soak for 6–8 hours)
½ cup fat-free curd, made
   from 100 ml fat-free milk
   (0–0.8% fat)
4 large garlic cloves
2–3 green chillies, chopped
   coarsely
1 tbsp vinegar
4 tsp butter
1 tbsp oil

1 Pressure-cook the chickpeas in 3 cups of water with
   ½ tsp salt for 7–8 whistles. Strain and cool.
2 Grind the chickpeas to a paste in a blender with curd,
   garlic, green chillies, vinegar and salt. The paste should
   be of thick consistency.
3 Heat oil. Add carrots, cabbage and salt. Sauté for
   2–3 minutes. Set aside.
4 Slice off crusts of the bread. Using a rolling pin, flatten
   each slice as much as possible.
5 With a butter knife, spread 2 tbsp of the chickpea paste
   on each flattened slice.
6 Next, sprinkle 2 tbsp of the vegetable mixture over it.
7 Tightly roll each slice and apply a small amount of butter
   on all the exposed sides of the roll.
8 Roast in a non-stick pan, rolling from time to time, until
   evenly golden brown.
9 To serve, cut each roll into 3 pieces using a pizza cutter.
10 Serve with Green Chutney (recipe on page 152) and
   tomato ketchup.

VALUE PER SERVING		
	Calories	227 kcal
	Protein	7 gms
	Fat	7 gms
	Carbs	33 gms
	Calcium	136 mgs
	Fibre	1 gm
	Iron	1 mg

⏳ Quick & Easy

DESSERTS

MANGO PANEER ROLL

Please your sweet tooth with this low-fat,
low-sugar fresh fruit dessert

Makes: 12 rolls	Preparation time: 2 mins
Serving size: 2 rolls	Cooking time: 25 mins
Serves: 6	

600 ml double toned milk
  (1.5% fat)
2 tsp lemon juice
2 medium Alphonso mangoes
5 tsp powdered sugar

1 Bring milk to the boil and turn off flame. Immediately
   add lemon juice and stir until milk curdles. Strain through
   a muslin cloth, making sure all the liquid or whey is removed.
   What remains in the cloth is *paneer*.

2 Crumble the *paneer* and churn in a blender for 5–7 seconds
   while it is still hot. Remove into a flat plat and immediately
   add the powdered sugar. Mash thoroughly using your hand
   until completely smooth (approximately 5 minutes).

3 Divide into 12 parts and set aside.

4 Cut 12 thin, flat slices from the fullest part of the mangoes.

5 Place one part of the mashed *paneer* on the centre of
   each mango slice. Roll inwards, so that the mango envelopes
   the *paneer*.

6 Repeat for all 12 rolls.

7 Serve immediately or refrigerate.

VALUE PER SERVING		
	Calories	74 kcal
	Protein	3 gms
	Fat	1.5 gms
	Carbs	12 gms
	Calcium	122 mgs
	Fibre	0 gm
	Iron	0 mg

✳ Jain
❧ Gluten-free
⧗ Quick & Easy

Shelf life: Keep refrigerated and consume within 12 hours.

KESARIA SANDESH

Indulge in this sin-free take on the Bengali favourite

Makes: 8 pieces
Serving size: 1 piece
Serves: 8

Preparation time: 2 mins
Cooking time: 20 mins

1 litre toned milk (3.5% fat)
Juice of 1–1½ lemons
3 heaped tbsp powdered sugar
A few strands of saffron
2 tbsp hot toned milk (3.5% fat)

VALUE PER SERVING		
	Calories	107 kcal
	Protein	4 gms
	Fat	5 gms
	Carbs	11 gms
	Calcium	150 mgs
	Fibre	0 gm
	Iron	0.5 mg

1 Soak saffron in 2 tbsp hot milk.
2 Bring 1 litre of milk to the boil; turn off heat and add lemon juice. Stir until it curdles. If it does not curdle, add more lemon juice. Cover for two minutes. Strain through a muslin cloth, making sure all the liquid or whey is removed. What remains in the cloth is *paneer*.
3 Churn the *paneer* in a grinder while it is still hot. Add powdered sugar and grind again. Transfer to a smooth surface.
4 Mash by hand until a soft dough is formed and sugar is completely incorporated (approximately 5 minutes).
5 Divide the mixture into 8 equal parts and roll into balls. Using your finger, make a small depression in the centre of each ball and place a bit of the soaked saffron.
6 De-shell, de-skin and blanch 5–6 unsalted pistachios and chop them to use as a garnish along with the saffron (optional).
7 Refrigerate and served chilled.

✳ **Jain**
🍃 **Gluten-free**
⏳ **Quick & Easy**

Shelf life: Keep refrigerated and consume within 48 hours.

DUDHI HALWA with DRY FRUITS

A melt-in-your-mouth delight… so good
you'd never guess it's low in fat

Makes: 3 cups	Preparation time: 5 mins
Serving size: ½ cup	Cooking time: 35 mins
Serves: 6	

4 cups *dudhi* (bottle gourd), grated
1 litre fat-free milk (0–0.8% fat)
⅓ cup sugar
17 almonds, julienned
16 cashewnuts, julienned
½ tsp cardamom powder

1 Boil milk over a low flame, stirring constantly, till it reduces to half its quantity.

2 Squeeze *dudhi* to reduce the water content. Sauté in a non-stick pan for 2–3 minutes.

3 Cover the pan; steam for 10 minutes. Add the reduced milk, stirring constantly, and cook for 1 minute. Cover and cook for 5 minutes.

4 Stir in sugar, almonds and cashews; cook for 2 minutes or till *halwa* reaches a thick consistency. Remove from heat and add cardamom powder.

5 Serve hot or chilled.

VALUE PER SERVING	
Calories	156 kcal
Protein	7.5 gms
Fat	4.3 gms
Carbs	21.5 gms
Calcium	273 mgs
Fibre	0.6 gm
Iron	0.8 mg

✣ Jain
● Gluten-free

Shelf life: Keep refrigerated and consume within 24 hours.

APPLE ALMOND RABDI

A smooth, low-fat dessert flecked with bits
of apple, delicately laced with cinnamon

Makes: 2½ cups
Serving size: ½ cup
Serves: 5

Preparation time: 5 mins
Cooking time: 25 mins

20 almonds, sliced finely
1 litre double-toned milk
   (1.5% fat)
½ large apple
3 tbsp sugar
¼ tsp cinnamon powder

1 Boil milk till it reduces to half its quantity. Add sugar and
   boil for another 2 minutes.
2 Remove from flame; allow to cool.
3 Meanwhile, peel the apple and chop finely. Avoid chopping the
   apple beforehand as it tends to brown when exposed to air.
4 Stir chopped apple, almonds and cinnamon powder into the
   reduced milk.
5 Serve chilled.

VALUE PER SERVING		
Calories	152 kcal
Protein	7 gms
Fat	5 gms
Carbs	20 gms
Calcium	228 mgs
Fibre	0.2 gm
Iron	0.3 mg

✽ **Jain**
🍃 **Gluten-free**
⧖ **Quick & Easy**

Shelf life: Keep refrigerated and consume within 12 hours.

CHOCOLATE SANDESH

A ball of chocolaty goodness enveloped
by a layer of sweetened *paneer*

Makes: 12 halves	Cooking time: 15 mins
Serving size: 2 halves	
Serves: 6	

1 litre toned milk (3.5% fat)
Juice of 1 lemon
2 tbsp powdered sugar
2 tsp drinking chocolate

VALUE PER SERVING		
	Calories	135 kcal
	Protein	5 gms
	Fat	7 gms
	Carbs	13 gms
	Calcium	200 mgs
	Fibre	0 gm
	Iron	0 mg

1 Bring milk to the boil and turn off flame. Immediately add lemon juice and stir until milk curdles. Strain through a muslin cloth, making sure all the liquid or whey is removed. What remains in the cloth is *paneer*.

2 Grate *paneer* while it is still hot and add powdered sugar. Mash thoroughly, using your hand, until completely smooth (approximately 5–7 minutes).

3 Divide into 5 parts and set aside.

4 Take one part and add the drinking chocolate powder. Mix thoroughly (for approximately 1 minute). Divide this into 6 small parts and shape into round balls. These are your brown balls.

5 Combine the remaining 4 parts of *paneer*. Now divide this into 6 equal parts and shape each into a ball.

6 Flatten each white ball and place one brown chocolate ball in the centre. Cover from all sides and roll again into a smooth ball. This forms 1 *sandesh*.

7 Repeat for the remaining 5 white balls.

8 Refrigerate for 1 hour.

9 To serve, cut each *sandesh* into two halves with a buttered knife.

✳ Jain
🌑 Gluten-free
⌛ Quick & Easy

Shelf life: Keep refrigerated and consume within 12 hours.

BAKED GUD SANDESH

Oven-baked, jaggery-sweetened *paneer*
squares that are a guiltless indulgence

Makes: 10 portions
Serving size: 1 portion
Serves: 10

Preparation time: 0 mins
Cooking time: 20 mins

2 litres toned milk (3.5% fat)
Juice of 1 lemon
50 gms *gud* (jaggery), grated
6 almonds, chopped finely

1 Bring milk to the boil; turn off heat and add lemon juice.
   Stir until it curdles. If it does not curdle, add more lemon juice.
   Cover for 2 minutes. Strain through a muslin cloth, making
   sure all the liquid or whey is removed. What remains in the
   cloth is *paneer*.

2 Preheat the oven at 160°C for 7–10 minutes.

3 Grate the *paneer* and add the grated jaggery. Mash thoroughly,
   using your hand, until completely smooth, for approximately
   5–7 minutes.

4 Spread this mixture in an even layer, about half an inch thick,
   in a small baking dish.

5 Bake in preheated oven for approximately 10 minutes or
   until the surface turns golden brown.

6 Garnish with almonds. Divide into 10 equal portions and serve.

VALUE PER SERVING		
Calories	155 kcal
Protein	6 gms
Fat	8 gms
Carbs	13 gms
Calcium	260 mgs
Fibre	0 gm
Iron	0 mg

✳ Jain
● Gluten-free
⧗ Quick & Easy

Shelf life: Refrigerate any leftovers and consume within 12 hours.

FRUITY PRALINE YOGURT

Thick, creamy, sweetened yogurt punctuated with
crispy bits of fruit and crunchy praline

Makes: 3 cups
Serving size: ½ cup
Serves: 6

Pre-preparation time: 5 hrs
Preparation time: 2 mins
Cooking time: 10 mins

1 medium apple (or any other
    fruit of your choice)
5 cups fresh curd, made from
    1 litre toned milk (3.5% fat;
    hung for 5 hours)
6 almonds, chopped coarsely
3 tbsp crystallised sugar
3 tbsp powdered sugar
¼ tsp cinnamon powder

1 Grease a plate with a drop of *ghee* and set aside.
2 To make praline, heat 3 tbsp crystallized sugar in a pan,
   stirring continuously with a fork, until it melts and caramelised
   to a golden-brown liquid. Remove from heat and add almonds.
3 Immediately spread the praline mixture on the greased plate.
4 Once set and cooled completely, churn praline in a mixer for
   2 seconds. Set aside.
5 Strain the hung curd through a muslin cloth. Stir in cinnamon
   and powdered sugar.
6 Peel the apple and cut into fine cubes. Add to the
   sweetened curd.
7 Mix in ¾ of the praline. Refrigerate.
8 To serve, pour the fruit cream into 6 small cups and garnish
   each with the remaining praline. Serve chilled.

VALUE PER SERVING		
	Calories	180 kcal
	Protein	5 gms
	Fat	7 gms
	Carbs	23 gms
	Calcium	253 mgs
	Fibre	0 gm
	Iron	1 mg

✻ Jain
❧ Gluten-free

Shelf life: Keep refrigerated and consume within 48 hours.

STRAWBERRY SANDESH

Fresh strawberries wrapped in a sweet, *paneer*-based 'cream' – sinful on the lips, not the hips

Makes: 24 halves
Serving size: 2 halves
Serves: 12

Preparation time: 5 mins
Cooking time: 60 mins

2 litres toned milk (3.5% fat)
Juice of 2 lemons
6 tbsp powdered sugar
12 medium strawberries

1   Bring 2 litres of milk to the boil; turn off heat and add lemon juice. Stir until it curdles. If it does not curdle, add more lemon juice. Cover for 2 minutes. Strain through a muslin cloth, making sure all the liquid or whey is removed. What remains in the cloth is *paneer*.

2   Churn the *paneer* in a blender for 3 seconds. Transfer to a flat plate and while it is still hot, add powdered sugar.

3   Mash by hand until a soft dough is formed and sugar is completely incorporated (approximately 5 minutes). Deep freeze for 20 minutes.

4   Divide the mixture into 12 equal parts. Wrap each part around one strawberry, such that it takes the shape of the strawberry.

5   Refrigerate once again for 30–40 minutes. Slice each piece length-wise into half with a buttered knife. Serve chilled.

VALUE PER SERVING		
Calories	148 kcal
Protein	5 gms
Fat	7 gms
Carbs	16 gms
Calcium	204 mgs
Fibre	0 gm
Iron	1 mg

✳ Jain
🍃 Gluten-free

Shelf life: Keep refrigerated and consume within 48 hours.

CHEENA PAIS

A creamy, fruity, milk-based dessert
that's rich to taste but low on calories

Makes: 3½ cups
Serving size: ⅓ cup
Serves: 10

Preparation time: 5 mins
Cooking time: 30 mins

2 litres toned milk (3.5% fat)
4 tbsp sugar
Juice of 1 lemon
2 cups pomegranate (or any
  other seasonal fresh fruit)

1 Pour 1 litre of milk each in two separate pans. Start heating
   both simultaneously.
2 Boil the milk in the first pan until it reduces to a little less than
   half its quantity (400 ml). Add sugar and continue heating for
   1 minute.
3 When the milk in the second pan comes to the boil, turn
   off the flame. Immediately add lemon juice, stirring until
   milk curdles. Strain and add to the reduced milk in the first
   pan. Remove from heat and stir well. Cool completely.
4 Add the fruit of your choice (preferably pomegranate,
   strawberry, grapes or mango). Serve chilled.

VALUE PER SERVING		
Calories	187 kcal
Protein	8 gms
Fat	8 gms
Carbs	20 gms
Calcium	313 mgs
Fibre	1 gm
Iron	0 mg

✳ Jain
● Gluten-free
⌛ Quick & Easy

Shelf life: Keep refrigerated and consume within 24 hours.

DATE FUDGE

A gooey, buttery dessert of date and coconut,
dusted with powdered coconut

Makes: 10 pieces	Preparation time: 10 mins
Serving size: 2 pieces	Cooking time: 10 mins
Serves: 5	

100 gms dates, after de-seeding
5 Marie biscuits
3 tbsp dried coconut powder
1 tbsp butter

1   Cut the dates into thin, long strips. Keep aside.
2   Break the biscuits into small pieces (1 biscuit into
    approximately 20 pieces).
3   Heat the butter in a pan. Add the chopped dates and sauté
    for 2–3 minutes. Stir in 1 tbsp of the coconut powder.
    Sauté for 10–15 seconds, then turn off the flame.
4   While the date mixture is still hot, add the crushed biscuits
    and mix thoroughly (for about 2 minutes).
5   Divide the mixture into 10 equal parts. Shape each part
    into a ball and flatten slightly.
6   Roll each piece separately in the remaining 2 tbsp
    of coconut powder.
7   Serve immediately or refrigerate.

VALUE PER SERVING		
	Calories	120 kcal
	Protein	1 gm
	Fat	4 gms
	Carbs	19 gms
	Calcium	40 mgs
	Fibre	1 gm
	Iron	2 mgs

✳ Jain
⧗ Quick & Easy

Shelf life: Refrigerate any leftovers and consume within 4 days.

BANOFFEE PIE

A spin-off from the original – a biscuit base topped with condensed milk and banana, swapping whipped cream for custard

Makes: 1 pie (6 slices)	Preparation time: 5 mins
Serving size: 1 slice	Cooking time: 20 mins
Serves: 6	

8 Marie biscuits
1 large banana
½ cup condensed milk
1 tsp cocoa powder
3 tsp powdered sugar
300 ml fat-free milk (0–0.8% fat)
4 tsp custard powder
3 whole walnuts, chopped finely
1 tbsp melted butter

1 Preheat oven to 120°C/250°F.
2 Crush the biscuits and grind in a blender for 5 seconds. Remove and mix it with melted butter, 1 tbsp water and walnuts.
3 Spread the mixture evenly on the base of an ovenproof medium-sized baking dish (6" to 8" in diameter).
4 Bake crust for 7–10 minutes. Cool completely.
5 Pour the condensed milk over the biscuit layer and spread evenly.
6 Cut the banana into ¼-inch-thick slices and arrange them over the layer of condensed milk.
7 Heat 200 ml of milk until it comes to the boil. Meanwhile, dissolve 4 tsp custard powder in the remaining 100 ml of milk.
8 Add the custard mixture to the boiling milk. Continue to cook over low heat, stirring constantly, until the milk thickens. Stir in sugar and set aside until it reaches room temperature. Pour custard evenly over the banana layer. Dust the top with cocoa powder.
9 Refrigerate for 2–3 hours. Serve chilled.

VALUE PER SERVING		
	Calories	160 kcal
	Protein	4 gms
	Fat	4 gms
	Carbs	26 gms
	Calcium	82 mgs
	Fibre	0 gm
	Iron	0 mg

⌛ **Quick & Easy**

Shelf life: Keep refrigerated and consume within 48 hours.

SHAHI TUKDA

Saffron syrup-soaked bread drenched
with a sweetened milk reduction

Makes: 16 pieces
Serving size: 2 pieces
Serves: 8

Cooking time: 30 mins

4 slices white bread
750 ml toned milk (3.5% fat)
750 ml fat-free milk (0–0.8% fat)
½ cup sugar (for syrup)
4 tsp sugar (for milk)
12 almonds, julienned
1 tsp saffron
2 tsp *ghee*

1   Combine both types of milk. Bring to the boil; continue to
    simmer, stirring occasionally, until reduced to ¼ the quantity.
2   Meanwhile, for the syrup, bring 1½ cup of water to the boil
    and add ½ cup sugar. Simmer till the sugar melts completely.
3   Remove from heat and add saffron. Set aside to cool.
4   Preheat the oven at 160°C for 7–10 minutes.
5   Apply ½ tsp *ghee* on each slice of bread. Cut each slice
    into quarters; toast all 16 pieces in preheated oven for
    5–7 minutes until evenly browned.
6   Add 4 tsp sugar to the reduced milk and cook for another
    minute. Remove from heat and allow to cool.
7   Dip each toasted bread piece in the sugar syrup and arrange
    on a serving dish.
8   Just before serving, pour the reduced milk over the
    bread pieces.
9   Garnish with almonds. Serve immediately.

VALUE PER SERVING		
Calories	183 Kcal
Protein	7 gms
Fat	6 gms
Carbs	25 gms
Calcium	229 mgs
Fibre	0 gm
Iron	0 mg

✳ **Jain**

Shelf life: Keep refrigerated and consume within 12 hours.

ENGLISH – HINDI GLOSSARY

A

All purpose flour (super-refined flour) – Maida
Almonds – Badam
Aniseed – Saunf
Apple – Seb
Asafoetida – Hing

B

Baby corn – Chote bhutte
Banana – Kela
Basic whole-wheat unleavened flat bread, roti – Chapati
Basil – Tulsi patta
Bay leaves – Tej patta
Bell pepper/capsicum – Shimla mirch
Bengal gram, split – Chana dal
Bengal gram, whole – Chana
Black gram, split – Urad dal
Black gram, whole – Whole urad
Black pepper powder – Kaali mirch ka powder
Black peppercorns – Sabut kali mirch
Black salt – Kala namak
Black-eyed peas – Chowli beans
Bottle gourd – Dudhi
Bread, flat, girdle fried – Paratha
Brinjal – Baingan
Broccoli – Hari phool ghobi
Broken wheat – Dalia/lapsi
Butter – Makhan
Buttermilk – Chaas

C

Cabbage – Patta gobhi
Cardamom – Elaichi
Carom seeds – Ajwain
Carrots – Gajar
Cashewnuts – Kaju
Cauliflower – Phool ghobi
Celery – Ajwan ka patta
Chickpeas/garbanzo beans – Kabuli chana/chole
Chole powder, ready to use – Chole masala
Churned yogurt – Lassi
Cinnamon – Dalchini
Cloves – Lavang
Coconut – Nariyal
Condensed milk – Sanaghanit dudh/khova
Coriander leaves – Hara dhania
Corn – Makai
Corn flour – Makai ka atta
Corn from the cob – Sabut bhutte ke daane
Cottage cheese – Paneer
Croutons – Bread ke tukde, seke hue
Cucumber – Kakdi
Cumin seeds – Jeera
Curd/yogurt – Dahi
Curry leaves – Meetha neem patta/kari patta

D

Dates – Khajur
Dew gram – Moth/matki
Dough – Goonda hua atta

E

Egg – Anda

F

Fenugreek – Methi
Fenugreek leaves – Methi patta
Fenugreek leaves (dried) – Kasuri methi
Figs, dried – Sukhe anjeer
French beans – Fansi

G

Gambages; Garcinia indica – Kokum
Garlic – Lehsun
Ginger – Adrak
Ginger-chilli paste – Peesa hua adrak
    aur hari mirch
Gram flour – Besan/chana atta
Grapes – Angoor
Green chilli – Hari mirch
Green gram without skin – Yellow moong dal
Green gram, split – Hari moong dal
Green gram, sprouted – Ankurit moong
Green gram, whole – Moong
Green peas – Hare matar
Green peas, dried, field – Hara vatana
Ground mixture of hot and tangy spices –
    Garam masala
Ground mixture of tangy spices – Chaat masala

H

Honey – Shehad

I

Iron griddle or pan – Tawa

J

Jaggery – Gud

K

Kashmiri chilli – Kashmiri lal mirch
Kidney beans – Rajma

L

Legume soup – Dal
Lemon – Nimbu
Lentils, red whole – Masoor dal
Lettuce – Salad patta/kasmisaag

M

Mango – Aam
Mango powder, raw – Amchur powder
Milk – Dudh
Milo/Sorghum vulgare – Jowar/juar/jwari
Mint leaves – Pudina ke patte
Mushrooms – Kumbh/kukur mutta
Mustard powder – Pisi hui rai ka powder
Mustard seeds – Rai

N

Nutmeg – Jaiphal

O

Oat bran – Jai ka bhusa
Oatmeal/oats – Jav/jai/vilaiti jaun
Oil – Khane ka tel
Okra – Bhindi
Olive oil – Zaitoon ka tel
Olives – Zetoon/zaitoon
Onion – Pyaj/kanda
Onion seeds/nigella – Kalonji
Orange – Santra
Oregano – Ajwain

P

Papaya – Papita
Paprika – Lal mirch ka chura
Parsley – Achumooda
Patty, minced food – Tikki
Pav bhaji powder, ready to use –
Pav bhaji masala
Peach – Aarhoo/satalu
Peanuts – Sing dana
Pepper – Kali mirch
Pigeon peas, split – Tuvar dal
Pine nuts – Chilgoza
Pistachios – Pista
Pomegranate seeds – Anardana
Pomegranate – Anar
Poppy seeds – Khus khus
Potato – Aloo
Puffed rice – Kurmura
Pumpkin – Petha

R

Radish – Mooli
Raisin – Kishmish
Red bell pepper – Lal Shimla mirch
Red chilli flakes – Lal mirch ka chura
Red chilli powder – Lal mirch powder
Red chillies, dried – Sukhi lal mirch
Red Kasmiri chillies, dried – Kashmiri mirch
Rendered butter – Ghee
Rice – Chawal
Rice, long grain – Basmati chawal
Ridge gourd – Turai/toru
Rock salt – Kala namak

S

Saffron – Kesar
Salt – Namak

Sambhar powder, ready to use – Sambhar masala
Semolina – Rawa/sooji
Sesame seeds – Safed til
Sour curd – Khatta dahi
Spinach – Palak
Spring onion – Hara kanda
Sprouts – Ankurit moong/moth
Sugar – Shakkar
Sweet corn kernels – Bhutte ke daane
Sweet lime – Mosambi

T

Tamarind – Imli
Tofu – Soya paneer
Tomato – Tamatar
Tomato ketchup – Tamatar ka sauce
Turmeric – Haldi

V

Vinegar – Sirka

W

Walnuts – Akhrot
Watermelon – Kalingar
Wheat – Gehoon
Wheat flour – Gehoon ka atta
White peas, dried – Safed vatana
Wok – Kadai

Y

Yellow bell pepper – Peeli Shimla mirch
Yellow corn flour/maize flour – Makai ka atta

Z

Zucchini – Ek prakar ki kakdi

BIBLIOGRAPHY

Gopalan,C., Rama Sastri, B.V., Balasubramanian, S.C. Nutritive Value of Indian foods. Hyderabad, India: National Institute of Nutrition, Indian Council of Medical Research, 1971

Mahan, Kathleen L., Stump-Escott, Sylvia. Krause's *Food nutrition and Diet Therapy.* USA: Saunders, Elsevier, 2004.

Snowdown, Les., Humphreys Maggie. *Fitness Walking.* Delhi, India: Orient Paperbacks, 1997.

Willcox, Bradley J., Willcox, Craig D., Suzuki Makoto. The Okinawa Program. New York: Clarkson Potter/Publishers, 2001.

Online Resources
www.caloriecount.com
www.tracker.dailyburn.com
www.myfitnesspal.com

CONTACT SELFCARE

Tardeo | Head office
432/433 Arun Chambers,
Tardeo Main Road, Mumbai 400034
T: +9122 6131 2222 | F: +9122 6131 2200
M: +91 98197 25207
Hours: 9.30 am – 5.30 pm Monday – Friday
        9.30 am – 1.30 pm Saturday

Santacruz
302 Golden Bunglow, Juhu Road,
Opp. Santacruz Police Station,
Santacruz (W), Mumbai 400054
T: +9122 2661 3119
Hours: 9.30 am – 5.30 pm Monday, Wednesday & Friday
        9.30 am – 1.30 pm Saturday

Kolkata
238 A, Trinity Plush, Unit C, 1st floor,
AJC Bose road ,Kolkata 700020
T: +9133 6457 1113 | M: +91 93395 64578
Hours: 10 am – 5.30 pm Monday – Friday
        10 am – 2 pm Saturday

**We also offer online programs so you can avail
of our services from anywhere in the world.**

For further information
Call: +9122 6131 2222
Email: care@selfcareindia.com
Visit: **www.selfcareindia.com**
Follow: **www.facebook.com/selfcarebysuman**

JAICO PUBLISHING HOUSE

ESTABLISHED IN 1946, Jaico Publishing House is home to world-transforming authors such as Sri Sri Paramahansa Yogananda, Osho, The Dalai Lama, Sri Sri Ravi Shankar, Robin Sharma, Deepak Chopra, Jack Canfield, Eknath Easwaran, Devdutt Pattanaik, Khushwant Singh, John Maxwell, Brian Tracy and Stephen Hawking.

Our late founder Mr. Jaman Shah first established Jaico as a book distribution company. Sensing that independence was around the corner, he aptly named his company Jaico ('Jai' means victory in Hindi). In order to service the significant demand for affordable books in a developing nation, Mr. Shah initiated Jaico's own publications. Jaico was India's first publisher of paperback books in the English language.

While self-help, religion and philosophy, mind/body/spirit, and business titles form the cornerstone of our non-fiction list, we publish an exciting range of travel, current affairs, biography, and popular science books as well. Our renewed focus on popular fiction is evident in our new titles by a host of fresh young talent from India and abroad. Jaico's recently established Translations Division translates selected English content into nine regional languages.

Jaico's Higher Education Division (HED) is recognized for its student-friendly textbooks in Business Management and Engineering which are in use countrywide.

In addition to being a publisher and distributor of its own titles, Jaico is a major national distributor of books of leading international and Indian publishers. With its headquarters in Mumbai, Jaico has branches and sales offices in Ahmedabad, Bangalore, Bhopal, Bhubaneswar, Chennai, Delhi, Hyderabad, Kolkata and Lucknow.